Benedición

The Complete Poetry of Tato Laviera

TATO LAVIERA

PREFACE BY
Nicolás Kanellos

INTRODUCTION BY
Laura Lomas

Arte Público Press
Houston, Texas

Bendición is made possible through a grant from the City of Houston through the Houston Arts Alliance. We are grateful for their support.

Recovering the past, creating the future

Arte Público Press
University of Houston
4902 Gulf Fwy, Bldg 19, Rm 100
Houston, Texas 77204-2004

Cover design by Giovanni Mora

Laviera, Tato.
    [Poems. Selections]
    Bendición : the complete poetry of Tato Laviera / by Tato Laviera ; preface by Nicolás Kanellos ; introduction by Laura Lomas.
        p. cm.
    ISBN 978-1-55885-800-8 (alk. paper)
    I. Title.
    PS3562.A849A6 2014
    811'.54—dc23
                                            2014029890
                                            CIP

14 15 16 17 18 19 20   10 9 8 7 6 5 4 3 2 1

Contents

MAINSTREAM ETHICS   135

MIXTURAO AND OTHER POEMS   265

Preface

In November 1979, I published the foreword to Tato Laviera's first book, *La Carreta Made a U-Turn*. Little did I know then that Tato's untimely death at age 54 would still the wheels of Tato's *carreta* and lead to my writing one final preface, this time to his complete poems. "Complete." It sounds so final, but in truth there is no finality to Tato's contribution, his vision, his embrace not only of readers but of all who were fortunate to know him and be touched by his genius. My relationship with Tato reaches back to the early seventies, when he invited me into the air shaft behind Miguel Algarín's Lower East Side apartment and recited almost totally from memory about an hour-and-a-half of his poems. From then on, we forged a close friendship and working relationship in which we planned out the publication of his poetry and, after the founding of Arte Público Press, the issuing of his first book. But even before that, we had begun publishing Tato's works in our magazine, *Revista Chicano-Riqueña*, so that when *La Carreta Made a U-Turn* was published, there was already a growing awareness among Latino readers of Tato's poetry and plays and, of course, of his oral performances in New York City.

I think of Tato not only as a Hemispheric writer, one who represents the forging of new culture from the diverse peoples to be found from Tierra del Fuego to Alaska, but also as the quintessential New York poet, who embraced and sought to celebrate Latinos, yes, but also Russians, Jews, Italians, Asians, Afro-Americans and everyone who made up his beloved city. He eulogizes artists of many backgrounds, such as "suni paz," "miriam makeba," John Lennon in "john forever" and Ismael Rivera in "el sonero mayor" and pays his respects to the poetic vision of everyday people, their pride and toughness, adopting their voices in such poems as "juana bochisme," "esquina dude," "olga pecho" and "maría ciudad." And unlike many male writers of his generation, Tato indicted machismo—see his poem "machista"—and foregrounded the strong women of the barrio, maintaining their integrity and sense of pride, as in "compañero," engaging

in the battles to preserve neighborhoods and culture as in "the suffering of ruth santiago sánchez" which was dedicated to his indomitable
sister. Tato commanded respect for our women, but more importantly,
they speak for themselves through his verse:

> look here, brother, you cannot control me,
> so, don't even try, I have too many options
> to be convinced by your guajiro
> back-dated menaces or your semi-jealousies,
> whatever you say, I am not buying macho talk. (158)

If there is anyone conspicuously absent from Tato's cosmology it
is those New Yorkers who reign in board rooms and penthouses, the
"one-percenters" who ignore or disdain the lives that command Tato's
and our attention and compassion. Tato focuses fifty stories below to
his fellow street-level survivors, hailing from all parts of the world and
struggling to eke out a living in cramped sweatshops, dank factories,
steamy kitchens or in the cacophony and miasma of the streets. The
streets . . . the streets that Tato loved so much, that he covered endlessly
with his nervous, fast pace, so much so that he perennially had holes in
his soles . . . the streets where he engaged with what sociologist might
call the grassroots and literati might refer to as *der volk,* from which he
gained so much inspiration and whose inhabitants he treated as worthy
subjects for what Tato saw as the highest art: Poetry with a capital P.

Tato has been studied as a Nuyorican poet, although he was born in
Puerto Rico and received his early schooling there. He is seen as a
black poet and a cultivator of "jazz poetry" and Afro-Caribbean themes,
although his corpus goes far beyond these specific motifs and styles. He
is seen as a Latino poet, even before the term became generalized, and
although he reached out to Chicanos and Cubans and Central and South
Americans, he never promoted the term "Latino." He is hailed as an
oral poet par excellence, despite his having published five books of
poems. He was all of these and much more; his verse, like his penetrating gaze, challenged the reader to come to terms with his expansive
and apparently elusive identity, similar to the challenge proposed in his
famous poem "tito madera smith":

> you can call him tito,
> or you can call him madera,

or you can call him smitty,
or you can call him mr. t,
or you can call him nuyorican,
or you can call him black,
or you can call him latino,
or you can call him mr. smith,
his sharp eyes of awareness,
greeting us in aristocratic harmony:
"you can call me many things, but
you gotta call me something." (94)

It is just that yearning to be called something, to be recognized not just as part of American identity, but to be really accepted as the epitome of what it means to be American, that forces us to confront how authorities and their institutions have reduced and marginalized what is most vital in our national make-up. And Tato ALWAYS challenged that marginalization. In his demand for centrality, he confronted "Lady Liberty" and sought to re-define "American":

. . . i love this, my second
land, and i dream to take the accent from
the altercation, and be proud to call
myself american, in the u.s. sense of the
word, AmeRícan, America! (263)

However, he will only remove the accent mark from his Rican-inflected Americanism if and when we integrate the nation and define our "own destino, our own way of life, (. . .) defining the new america, humane america, / admired america, loved America" (262). And while Tato may have given voice to the ambivalence and confusion in the cultural lives of all diasporic peoples in his book *Mixturao and Other Poems,* and specifically in his call-and-response poem "nideaquinideallá," Tato never ended on a pessimistic note, his poetry foreseeing a future of political and economic triumph and the flourishing of our culture. No, never pessimistic, his poetry was a call for all of us to participate in realizing those dreams.

In his expansiveness, Tato was nothing if not a poet of love, but I always saw that love as embracing the common folk, extending to our enemies, his love as an appreciation for the tribe, the nation, the city

. . . As Tato was preparing his works for publication—silly me—I told him that in this day and age it is almost impossible to write an original and un-trite love poem. He took the challenge, stating that he'd write three that I could not help but publish. Furthermore, he promised, they'd be so good that young dudes in the neighborhoods would carry them around in their back pockets, ready to be removed and read to their "squeezes" with pride (even if plagiarized from him). He held to his word and produced what I can only say are the most original, sensual, erotic, feminist poems of love that I have read in contemporary literature (and they are bilingual at that!): "just before the kiss," "velluda: alliterated y eslembao" and "standards."

But, you say, what about those poems of flaming anger, such as "angelitos' eulogy in anger" and "simplemente maría"? In those lyric outbursts of frustration and protest, in tones quite often associated with Latino literature of the civil rights movements, Tato does not lend his voice to any specific ideology other than expressing deep wounds as experienced in the flesh by his mother, his brother and himself, and of course his desire to fight oppression. And it is out of love that he must anger and shout and attack the systems that have dehumanized and exploited those close to him and, by extension, himself.

mami, tears of sacrifice sanctify
your delicate face, valley of tears
in your heart
mami, I love you
the spirit of love gives me rancor
and hate, and I react to the song
simplemente maría, but my anger
my hate
is based on love, ultimate love of you!

mami, you are my epitome
but I shall be your sword (31)

And *Bendición: The Complete Poetry of Tato Laviera* is Arte Público Press' expression of enduring love for Tato and the love, insight, celebration, anger, music his poetry has contributed to our lives. May it live on.

Nicolás Kanellos
Publisher

"This is a Warning, My Beloved America": Tato Laviera and the Birth of a New American Poetic Language*

In Memoriam: Jesus Abraham Tato Laviera (1951-2013)

this is a warning, my beloved america.

so touch me,
and in touching me
touch all our people.

—Tato Laviera, "lady liberty"

Jesús Abraham "Tato" Laviera's poetry performs ways to overcome the multiple forces that divide those of us living inside empire. The poetic corpus offers a blessing and a challenge to help with this difficult task. For to receive Laviera's *bendición* places the reader on a "camino-carrito-cultural" ("doña cisa y su anafre"), tasting the delicate flavor of *dignidad* and feeling the welcoming handshake of affirmation and expectation. Infused with generosity, sacrifice, anger and invitations to *rumbear*, these pages speak from

---

*Mil gracias a Nicolás Kanellos for opening the door, and to Tato Laviera, for inviting me in. Thanks to my inspiring students at Rutgers Newark for comments on this introduction.

and to the place of "the person / in this society most likely to suffer . . . " ("para ti, mundo bravo"). Studying the complex and intersecting layers of colonization, genocide, slavery and their contemporary legacies, Laviera turns to *las costumbres que son la base del pueblo,* the quotidian philosophy, rhythm and *chisme* that have made it possible to survive and to remake this "uprooted temperate zone" ("social club," "conciencia" "against muñoz pamphleteering"). Laviera's poetry makes audible the voices—from the streets in front of abandoned buildings in Loisaida to the Supreme Court of the United States—that focus on the "tiny ray / of sun struggling to sneak in . . . a new freedom which said, 'we are / beautiful anywhere, you dig?'" ("a tight touch" "i am a wise latina"). To receive this blessing prompts an answer, like the call-and-response structure of the poems; for Tato defines an ethics, *un camino,* or a way of talking and walking. Tato will haunt us, until we make good on the expectations he has of we who read him, and of our America.

Laviera's complete poems depict a poet seeking liberation through the creation of a new language and new poetic forms. Expanding upon a tradition of New York sojourners that extends back through Julia de Burgos, Langston Hughes and José Martí, Laviera has earned a place alongside the greatest American poets, in the broadest sense of that term. By reclaiming Spanglish, a language they taught us to despise (Cliff), Laviera refuses to assimilate to monolingualist, white supremacist confusion and perfumed academic arrogance ("bochinche bilingüe"). Whoever you are holding Tato now in hand, remember that in the tradition of Walt Whitman's invitation-warning, there is much you won't fully understand. But rather than feel excluded, please read here an invitation: to grasp more by becoming bilingual, to hear more by studying literature not only by reading books, to feel more by experiencing spirits goofing with you ("subway song") or to respect more by honoring our forerunners ("homenaje a don luis palés matos"). Laviera's poetry makes sense of a Latin American and Caribbean diasporic tradition in what is now the United States, and points toward a future mainstream ethics that affirms social justice, access and cultural impurity as the lasting contribution of the Latina/o majority America. We who read *Bendición*—like the poet, like his America—"still ha[ve] plenty of room / to grow" ("para ti, mundo bravo").

Against Amnesia in Loisaida and Beyond

Although not part of the first 1975 anthology of Nuyorican poetry edited by Miguel Algarín and Miguel Piñero, Tato figures in Algarín and Bob Holman's *Aloud: Voices from the Nuyorican Poet's Café* and becomes an exemplary figure of the Nuyorican movement while also assuming a trajectory beyond the café in its pre- and post-Piñero "slam" phases, and beyond the Loisaida community of his origins. Like other Nuyorican poets, Laviera vents spiritual anger at the ghetto conditions of the 1970s and 1980s Lower East Side, when his neighborhood was a place of swollen-belly *hambre* and *frío*, of broken steam heat due to landlord neglect and nefarious urban blight. His poems document the extent to which twentieth-century New York City was full of "eighteenth-century abandoned structures" ("suffering of ruth santiago sánchez"), by which we can understand both old tenements and exclusionary social forms that characterized life before the Haitian, French and North American revolutions. With the worst segregation of public schools in the nation (even more than before *Brown vs. Board of Education*) and the bitter absence of Spanish-English dual-language schools in Loisaida's District One, gentrification has displaced and does not serve most Latina/o and other working-class residents. Our United States of amnesia runs the risk of forgetting the legacy of the Nuyorican poets to its great loss as Uroyoán Noel has eloquently argued, despite the fact that E. 3rd Street bears the name of Reverend Pedro Pietri (*In Visible Movement*). (We ask: Where is the street for Tato Laviera?). New York and the country have not adequately redistributed health nor wealth, nor affirmatively acted to redress racism.

A direct effect of this amnesia is that Tato Laviera became homeless in 2010, precisely when he should have been enjoying a university position, the honors of a poet laureate or at least health benefits and affordable housing (Gonzalez, "Poet Spans Two Worlds but has a Home in Neither"). This shameful fact suggests that Laviera's critique of the rotten hollow laughter of illusory progress, the disorienting silence, mutilated phrases and frozen syllables ("conciencia") remains incisive. Laviera's warnings about ruthless economic disparities, unequal education, self-degradation and against corrupt politics still ring true.

Laviera's metaphor of language as a weapon—*la ametralladora de la libertad*—to transform consciousness suggests, following

Mohammed Alí, that writing is fighting. Writing can give the working-class majority of color—who tend to be most underserved by public education—a fighting chance. Like his nineteenth-century *independentista* precursors, Laviera sought to unite groups who were divided for the wrong reasons. For example, while he says he will fight for Puerto Rico, he calls the island to account for failing to recognize its diaspora: "me desprecias, me miras mal, me atacas mi hablar" ("nuyorican"). He forges links across the island/diaspora divide with the rhetorical invitation to know: "¿sabes?"

An Afro-Latino Anti-Assimilationist Hip to Intersectionality

Tato's "three-way warning poems" offer an extended meditation on the invisibility of the "moreno puertorriqueño" unnamed or blamed by nationalist and Marxist theoretical positions, which Tato develops further in "spanglish carta," dedicated to the Mexican-based exiled Puerto Rican cultural theorist and fiction writer José Luis González (1926-1996). In *AmeRícan's* section entitled "Nuyorican," the "three-way warning" poem evokes the Afro-Puertorriqueño's invisibility with two columns of syllables focusing on the divisions between Nuyorican and Puertorriqueño. *La Carreta's* "three-way warning" evokes an ongoing problem of nationalist discourses that silence or make blackness invisible. The poet directs himself to three audiences: 1) *blancos* performing in blackface the roles of *negros*, 2) *blancos* blaming *negros* for national and diasporic problems, such as the so-called degradation of the language, (René Marqués' "Puertorriqeño dócil") and, 3) *negros* who perpetuate the mental slavery of "no te juntes con los prietos, negrito," which is to say of assimilation to white attitudes and rejection of black solidarity, on the island and the mainland ("negrito").

Laviera explodes the binaries that often cancel out the perspectives of people of color living in the fissures or overlapping spaces of these categories, thus making a contribution to an influential woman of color feminist project limned by his contemporaries Gloria Anzaldúa, Audre Lorde and Kimberle Crenshaw. As to the binaries of Puerto Rican/Nuyorican, white/black, African-American/Latina/o, monolingual/bilingual, English/Spanish, populist/*independentista,* male/female, educated/uneducated, Laviera interjects black-affirming and feminist performative speech: "ay baramba bamba / suma acaba / quimbombo de salsa / la rumba matamba" ("el moreno puertorriqueño")—to affirm the spaces of Africanization, emergence and mixture that call into question theses hierarchies and structures of blame. The Afro-Latina/o space further elaborated in "tesis de negreza" refuses an extensive lexicon of pejorative Spanish-language labels for black people by breaking down the reductive logic that blames anti-black violence on blackness, rather than on white perpetrators and institutions. Laviera responds by affirming the blackness of his poetic persona, naming *bomba* as *raíz*, and revealing "the root called africa in all of us" ("the salsa of bethesda fountain").

Laviera's poetic celebration of untranslatable Puerto Rican speech, too black to be translated or assimilated (as in "asimilao") offers a creative alternative to the prevailing expectations of migrants to the United States, as Juan Flores, John Attinasi and Pedro Pedraza Jr. noted in 1981. Laviera's affirmation of the black "AO" documents the onomatopoeia exacted by the pressure to assimilate and provides an antidote at the same time, a strategy for which we must give thanks to los prietos who give us an original American language. Thus Laviera's poetry rightly becomes a key reference point for the *Afro-Latin@* tradition anthologized by Juan Flores and Miriam Jiménez Román in 2010. Perhaps Flores' generative shift from a class-centered theoretical framework in his early work to "diaspora from below" is in part thanks to Tato's *bendición*. Indeed, we might ask further: What of the debts of Pulitzer Prize-winning Afro-Latino Junot Díaz to Laviera? As Díaz has become highly acclaimed for his novels, stories and essays that draw on the resources of Spanish and English, the languages in which he thinks and writes simultaneously, critics should take note of Laviera's laying the groundwork for his artistic form in the 1980s. The publication of Laviera's *Bendición* becomes more urgent than ever in what Díaz calls the "Age of the Writing Program," for Laviera's transgressive bending of the rules of literary language exemplify the kinds of experiments that become less and less likely to enter literary history given the increased gatekeeping, the white-dominant culture of most programs and the potentially homogenizing effect of the M.F.A. credential as the condition for working as a professional writer (Díaz).

Laviera breaks ground not only in writing in what he calls "black language" in his interview with Carmen D. Hernández, but also in introducing a fiercely independent Latina subjectivity to many of his poems. Pablo Martínez Diente, in his interview with Tato Laviera in

2006, notes the significant presence of Laviera's sympathetic portrayal of feminine characters in fifty-five of his one hundred eighty-seven poems, which Laviera attributes to "an exile of my subconscious" and to his awareness of the need to be humble. Laviera becomes a scribe, an historian, a medium who so accurately listens in the *cocina,* and on the *esquina* that he captures the tone, defiance and the self-affirmation of "juana bochisme," "m'ija" and "brava" without ever patronizing. Laviera's "a message to our unwed women," "machista" and "compañero" articulate a feminist independence and concomitantly demand a new kind of *compañero.* These feminist voices reject outright the North American puritanical view of the body and defend women's right to create new generations without shame. Here Laviera amplifies ideas explored by William Carlos Williams, Luisa Capetillo and Julia de Burgos, ideas that resonate directly with the most advanced thinking of the global feminist movement emerging in the 1970s and 1980s. In this sense, Laviera was ahead of his time in avoiding the *machista* tone that characterized much civil rights or nationalist discourse of the period.

Political Strategist, Poetic Pedagogue and Public Intellectual

As a playwright, poet, public intellectual, an electrifying poetry workshop leader, who got his start as a community organizer, Laviera saw and affirmed the connection between poetics, politics and pedagogy. According to his collaborator, Elizabeth Colón, Tato's poetry drew its energy from "his participation in the community's struggle. . . . He deeply understood the need of people to participate in their future" (qtd. Gonzalez, "Tato Laviera, 63, Poet of Nuyorican School"). Laviera forged his revolution in poetic language in the fire of 1970s politics, an insufficiently studied aspect of Laviera's biography. Five years before publishing his first volume of poetry, Laviera was president of the New Jíbaro Democrats and promoted Latina and Latino candidates who went on to leadership roles in the district assembly. In the Lower East Side, Tato's territory since he first arrived to New York at age ten, Puerto Ricans were the dominant Latina/o group, in the midst of a mostly Eastern European left-of-center Jewish and Chinese neighborhood. Under the leadership of Petra Santiago, Laviera worked for the Association of Community Services Centers, and in that capacity he picketed, organized voter registration drives and convened open-air salsa sessions to create neighborhood associations, to launch Loisiada's carnival, to create day care centers, to gain more public housing and to hire a superintendent who instituted bilingual schools. According to Colón, Tato "was a very spiritual person. He suffers your problems. He felt what we were feeling."* In his work as a political organizer and teacher, Laviera fought alongside his community for the Jesús Papotes sitting on the stoops of abandoned buildings, surrounded by junkies, with nowhere to go.

Laviera's poetry gives voice to a movement that builds up from the "debris of the ghettos" and brings to harvest the literary history and communities of readers and listeners excavated through the reclaiming of historical Hispanic writing in what is now the United States from the sixteenth to the twentieth centuries (Algarín "Nuyorican Aesthetics"). The twinned birth of a bilingual Latina/o poetic form and the affirmation of Spanish as an American language emerge from a poet-teacher-activist in the tradition of organic intellectuals and *declamadores*. Laviera honors his teachers Jorge Brandon (the father figure of the Nuyorican poets, whom Laviera invokes in "declamación," "jorge brandon" and "don luis muñoz marín"), and before that the black Puerto Rican *declamador*, Juan Boria, both of whom belong to a long tradition of racially integrated education in the school of Rafael Cordero (Ferrer Canales).

Laviera narrates the arrival of his artistic self-consciousness in "fighting." The poet-speaker relates this awareness to his ability to use words as weapons in his work in the community, "dealing with / institutions on their own / word and logic turf." This poem both acknowledges and claims that power of his "uneducated prose," which landed him a job teaching writing at Rutgers's Livingston College, a living / learning educational experiment which was created in response to the Newark riots of 1967 and the Newark Puerto Rican riot of 1974. This early poem cites the far more significant role of ideological struggle than physical violence. Self-affirmation becomes the crucial first step and begins when the poet of "fighting" "decided to stop downgrading / myself as i fused my / energies to create, to strive, / to extend myself onto / the largest horizon." Like Jorge Brandon's lesson that "all of us are creative cocos" (the last line of

---

*Interview with Elizabeth Colón, October 16, 2014. Colón was one of the candidates Laviera promoted on the "Por los niños" slate as a means to introduce new leaders who might better represent the interests of the Puerto Rican immigrant community.

"fighting," which certainly finds an echo in Piri Thomas' assumption that "every child is born a poet"), Laviera's poem entitled "book" affirms the role of independent presses such as Arte Público in helping to legitimize and publicize Nuyorican poets as part of an intellectual tradition extending from the Bible, through Cervantes, Shakespeare, Jefferson, Nietzsche, Neruda and Pietri.

As a teacher, Laviera was dedicated to moving beyond the university to the *arrabal*, or urban slum, and from there to the *frontera* or borderlands where empire exacts violence with electric fences, racialized policing and crack or crystal methamphetamine. The complete trajectory of Laviera's poetry (1979-2008) shows an expanding definition of *nosotros* to include an increasingly heterogeneous and still exploited Spanish-speaking working-class migrants, ("sur americanos," "indigenous" and "southwest border trucos"), many of whom lack human and citizenship rights. Through his work in co-founding Cosecha Voices with Stephanie Alvarez at University of Texas Pan-American, many Mexican student migrant workers found their voice in Laviera's writing workshops (Alvarez and Martínez). When Laviera orchestrated a visit of student writers from Cosecha Voices to my class on Narratives of Migration in the Americas, he affirmed his migrant-worker students' and my students' stories of migration to New Jersey, as an extension of the same Latina/o literary tradition.

Untranslatable Mixturao: The Last New Latest Name

In redefining Nuyorican displacement in terms of a continental framework in his last volume, *Mixturao* (previously entitled "Continental"), Laviera speaks to America in the sense that Martí, Neruda and other Latin American and Caribbean writers have given it. Laviera's poem "nideaquinideallá" affirms the trans-American border space this new third-person-plural inhabits. In performances of this playful call-and-response poem, half the audience would shout "nideaquí" and the other half respond "nideallá." As the title of this poem constitutes a "last new latest name," Laviera follows Julia de Burgos, Malcolm X and Nicolás Guillén in casting off the inherited patronymics of slavery, patriarchy and colonization. Here the poetic subject engages in a transgressive self-naming that straddles the pure languages, racial divisions and first world/third world economics that national borders attempt to police:

nidequinideallá
impossible to blend
impossible to categorize
impossible to analyze
impossible to synthesize
our guerrilla cultural camouflage
survival linguistic construction
at emergency moment's notice
complex afirmaciones parametric
principles fermenting
secretive universal
garabatopandegato
continental yearnings
complex jerigonza
de mi hablar

This last name, *nidequinideallá*, rejects grammatical rules of spacing
and capitalization. It makes language retention and invention a guerrilla tactic, much as Samuel Huntington feared. Recalling the inven-
tive play of "jerigonza" (a kind of Spanish pig Latin) —a phrase from
his "juana bochisme" that recenters *el hablar popular* that provides
poetic rhythms to Laviera, just as Langston Hughes riffed on the
blues—Laviera calls for the re-molding and re-designing of the
decomposed body of liberty in a fashion that refuses to abide the com-
fortable overlap of America and empire. Suffering in a racialized body
without full citizenship in the United States teaches Latina/o subjects
to take issue with "watching our nation invading other nations without an invitation" ("nideaquínideallá").

Not only does Laviera launch the largest list of Latina/o literature
in the nation with Nicolás Kanellos, Gabriela Ventura, Carolina Vil-
larroel and Marina Tristán's Arte Público Press, but he also goes on to
become the best-selling Latino poet in the United States. His late
twentieth-century continental vision has helped scholars—and I wish
here to acknowledge my debt in particular—to understand that late
nineteenth-century Cuban and Puerto Rican anti-colonialists are also
innovators of Latina/o migrant poetry and prose, and as such, they
form an indispensable part of a trajectory of newly defined, continental American literary aesthetics. Louis Reyes Rivera (1945-1912), the

pan-Africanist New York Puerto Rican poet and historian, relates this little-known history to the Nuyorican spoken-word tradition in "Inside the River of Poetry" (2002). These connections become available in light of the ongoing excavation and recontextualization of late nineteenth-century Puerto Rican and Cuban poet-revolutionaries and activist educators (José Martí, Sotero Figueroa, Rafael Serra, Francisco Gonzalo "Pachín" Marín), and of early twentieth-century literary innovators (Luisa Capetillo, Jesús Colón, Julia de Burgos) whom we can now read as Laviera's Latina/o forebears.

Laviera saw how the Cuban José Martí's work narrates a story of Latina/o migrants staking a claim to participate in the definition of another America, much as Laviera respells the term "AmeRícan" to mark the still incompletely recognized contributions of Puerto Ricans, Chicanas/os and other Latina/os in the United States and the Americas. José Martí and other migrant Latina/os in Lower Manhattan who were plotting revolution, performing their poetry at evening gatherings of the Latina/o community and attending La Liga, the night school for Afro-Cubans and Afro-Puerto Ricans founded by Rafael Serra, express similar political and poetic preoccupations to Laviera, who directed University of the Streets a century later. Sotero Figueroa, and head of the Club Borinquén and editor of *Patria* after Martí stepped down, describes Martí in a manner that aptly fits Tato Laviera: "a good man, who educates the working person so that he can march consciously toward the conquest of his rights; a modest man, who is prodigious without ostentation, and who, like the best of exemplars . . . unites wills, does not hate nor speak ill, and tends to facilitate the arrival of justice where the palms are most beautiful, the sun most refulgent and flowers and fruits, most varied, sweet and juicy" (*Patria,* 16 April 1892; my translation; qtd in Carlos Ripoll, "Prólogo"). Laviera's little known Afro-Puerto Rican antecedent Francisco "Pachín" Martín wrote poetry and plays, designed the Puerto Rican flag, edited periodicals and exemplified the combination of poetry, politics and pedagogy that unites this new American poetic language to a broader process of social transformation (Patria Figueroa de Cifredo).

Like the José Martí and his multiracial and trans-American collaborators who dedicated their lives to organizing revolution, Tato issues a wake-up call and a warning to America to make its vision of liberty touch all our people. Tato knew as Martí did that "a vital idea set ablaze before the world at the right moment . . . can stop a fleet of battleships" ("Our America" 288). Laviera, too, committed himself to the most disenfranchised and could have said with Martí, "con los pobres de la tierra / quiero yo mi suerte echar" ("Versos Sencillos"). Laviera has become renowned for articulating an alternative to assimilation on the mainland, a view that Martí articulated in 1892, when in his prologue to his disciple Gonzalo de Quesada y Aróstegui's poetry chapbook, *Primera Ofrenda,* he affirms the Latina/o difference of a new generation of Hispanics growing up in the United States: "The Mexicans of California, after fifty years of living within the United States, do not want to be of the United States: they want to be Mexicans. You [Gonzalo], raised from your root in the North, preferred in its colleges, praised by its societies, and as the most pure expression of a nation—its youth—you know the futility, the impossibility, the disaster of acculturation; —and you are Cuban" ("Carta a Gonzalo Quesada"). Also like Martí, especially in his journalism of the 1890s, Laviera underscores resonances across urban Hispanic Afro-Caribbean borderlands of South Florida, the African-Americans terrorized by the Ku Klux Klan and the *indios, tejanos* and *californianos* who were forced to flee their homes or found themselves racialized as "greasers" after the United States annexed half of Mexico in 1848 (See Chapter 5, Lomas). Laviera's "southwest border trucos," which he recited with a heavy Chicano accent and desultory delight, supplements the classic vision of Martí's "To Cuba!" or "Al Extranjero." For if Martí reads the racializing of "Latins" as a call to return to the island to avoid the insults and dangers faced by the annexed, racialized migrant workers or the formerly enslaved, Laviera responds by attuning his poetry to the creativity of those with no option to return, or without a nation to return to.

Nosotros Verdadero, Poderoso, Lleno and Amoroso

The closing poem to *Mainstream Ethics (ética corriente)* defines a "we" that takes shape in a conversation between the poet and an intimate interlocutor, whom he addresses with the pronoun "tú," to create a true, powerful, plentiful and loving "we". These rhyming words (in the Spanish original) combine to define a critical, human and powerful collective into which Laviera inducts his audiences through performances of his poetry from "jesús papote" to "mixturao." This expanded *nosotros* reemerges in the title poem from his last volume, in which the poetic subject speaks in English, to echo the concluding lines of the epic poem that "defines" the author Jesús Abraham "Tato" Laviera and marks his conquest of "the verbiage of the English dictionary" and of his fifth-grade teacher in New York who told him he could not be named Jesus because he was black (Carmen Hernández 83). In "jesús papote" in 1981, Laviera's poetic "i" speaks *in utero* and narrates his own birth on Christmas. This unlikely divinity's birth also marks a new beginning for "we, nosotros," a new subject who comes to define a key motif of Laviera's poetry. This "we" foresees and blesses the "hispanic hemispheric majority," "respectful of spanish-english forms," "latinos million bicultural humanists," "spanish tongue culture older than english," "multi-ethnic black-brown-red in affirmations," "ghetto brothers black americans indians," "oral poets transcending 2 european forms . . . we stand at crossroads 21st-century new man" ("jesús papote"). Each of these prophetic poetic lines evokes major debates about America's literary future in this new century that have continued to rage in the decades after the publication of this poem in 1981. In this poem, Laviera directs his readers to "allow this spanish word to be understood." Arriving from the unlikely celestial barkings of a baby born into Loisaida's ghetto is a book that will bring about the birth of a new American language, a new America poetry, a new America:

> there is a puerto rican
> blessing universal to the world
> hear it is only for you
> ....BEN...DI ...CI...ÓN (89)

Works Cited

"Report: New York has Most Segregated Public Schools in USA." *USA Today* 27 March 2014.

Algarín, Miguel. "Nuyorican Aesthetics." Asela Rodríguez de Laguna, ed. *Images and Identities: The Puerto Rican in Two World Contexts*. New Brunswick: Transaction Books, 1987. 161-163.

——, and Bob Holman. *Aloud: Voices of the Nuyorican Poet's Café*. New York: H. Holt, 1994.

——, and Miguel Piñero. *Nuyorican Poetry: An Anthology of Puerto Rican Words and Feelings*. New York: Morrow, 1975.

Alvarez, Stephanie and José L. Martínez. "La palabra, conciencia y la voz: Tato Laviera and the Cosecha Voices Project at the University of Texas Pan-American," in Stephanie Alvarez and William Luis, Eds. *The AmeRícan Poet: Essays on the Work of Tato Laviera.* New York: Center for Puerto Rican Studies, 2014. 204-236.

Anzaldúa, Gloria. *Borderlands/La Frontera: The New Mestiza.* San Francisco: Aunt Lute Books, 1987.

Cliff, Michelle. *Claiming an Identity They Taught me to Despise.* Watertown, MA: Persephone Press, 1980.

Colón, Elizabeth. Unpublished Interview with Laura Lomas, October 16, 2014.

Crenshaw, Kimberle. "Mapping the Margins: Intersectionality, Identity Politics and Violence Against Women of Color." *Stanford Law Review* 43. 6 (1991): 1241-1299.

Díaz, Junot. "The MFA vs POC." *New Yorker* 30 April 2014.

Hernández, Carmen D. "Tato Laviera." *Puerto Rican Voices in English: Interviews with Writers.* New York: Praeger, 1997. 77-84.

Huntington, Samuel. "The Hispanic Challenge." *Foreign Policy* (March-April 2004): 30-45.

Ferrer Canales, José. "Evocación del Maestro Rafael Cordero." *Revista / Review Inter-Americana* 20.3-4 (1990): 36-47.

Figueroa de Cifredo, Patria. *Pachín Marín, héroe y poeta.* San Juan: Universidad de Puerto Rico, 1967.

Flores, Juan, John Attinasi, and Pedro Pedraza, Jr. "'La Carreta Made a U-Turn': Puerto Rican Language and Culture in the United States. *Daedalus* 110.2 (1981): 193-217.

Flores, Juan. *The Diaspora Strikes Back: Caribeño Tales of Learning and turning.* New York: Routledge, 2009.

Flores, Juan, and Miriam Jiménez Román. *The Afro-Latin@ Reader: History and Culture in the United States.* Durham: Duke University Press, 2010.

Gonzalez, David. "Poet Spans Two Worlds but has a Home in Neither." *New York Times* 12 February 2010.

—, "Tato Laviera, 63, Poet of Nuyorican School." *New York Times.* 5 November 2013.

Laviera, Tato. *la carreta made a U-turn.* Houston: Arte Público Press, 1979.

—. *Enclave.* Houston: Arte Público Press, 1981.

—. *AmeRícan.* Houston: Arte Público Press, 1985.

—. *Mainstream Ethics (ética corriente).* Houston: Arte Público Press, 1988.

—. *Mixturao and other poems.* IHouston: Arte Público Press, 2008.

Lomas, Laura. *Translating Empire: José Martí, Migrant Latino Subjects and American Modernities.* Durham: Duke University Press, 2008.

Lourde, Audre. "Age, Race, Class and Sex: Women Redefining Difference." Lorde, *Sister Outsider.* Berkeley: Crossing Press, 1984.

Marqués, René. *El puertorriqueño dócil: literatura y realidad psicológica.* Barcelona: Editorial Antillana, 1967.

Martí, José. *Selected Writings.* Trans. Esther Allen, Ed. Roberto González Echevarría. New York: Penguin Books, 2002.

—. "Carta A Gonzalo Quesada." in *Obras Completas.* La Habana: Editorial Ciencias Sociales, 1975. Vol 5, p.195.

Noel, Uroyoán. *In Visible Movement: Nuyorican Poetry from the Sixties to Slam.* Iowa City: University of Iowa Press, 2014.

Reyes Rivera, Louis. "Inside the River of Poetry" (2002). <http://www.inmotionmagazine.com>.

Ripoll, Carlos. "Prólogo." Sotero Figueroa, *La Verdad de la Historia.* Ed. Carlos Ripoll. San Juan: Instituto de Cultura Puertorriqueña, 1977.

La Carreta Made a U-turn

Metropolis Dreams

para ti, mundo bravo

in the final analysis
i am nothing but a historian
who took your actions
and jotted them on paper

therefore making you
the source, the strength,
the base of my inspirations

in the final analysis
i know that the person
in this society
most likely to suffer . . .

                is you, out there
                sometimes living the
                life of a wandering nomad
                to taste the breadcrumbs
                of survival . . .

one thing though,
if we ever meet
and you overpower me,
i would mention a book
by dostoevsky which
you have not read

and don't think because i passed
the evening junior high school
exam that i am more educated
than you

i still have plenty of room
to grow, check me out
and straighten me . . .
don't cliché me . . .
i might get angry now

but in the final analysis
i'll appreciate it, thank you

even then he knew

papote sat on the stoop
a social club   plays   che che colé
a pentecostal church sings   hallelujah
the sunday garbage   three days old
                    a burned car
yards full of junk   an addiction center
drunks on every   empty   milk box
velloneras   parties   screams
                             firecrackers
air   infected   with   summer heat
junkies of   all kinds   all ages
papote sat on the stoop
puerto rican flags   for patches in the asses
political   prisoners   posters   destroyed
no stars   no skies   no room to breathe
papote sat on the stoop
miseducated   misinformed
a blown-up belly   of   malnutrition
papote sat on the stoop
of an abandoned building
he decided to go nowhere

frío

35 mph winds
& the 10 degree
weather
penetrated the pores
of our windows
mr. steam rested for
the night
the night we most
needed him

everybody arropándose
on their skin blankets
curled-up like the embryo
in my mother's womb
a second death birth
called nothingness

& the frío made more
asustos in our empty
stomachs

        the toilet has not
        been flushed for
        three days

a tight touch

inside the crevice
deeply hidden in basement land
inside an abandoned building
the scratching rhythm of dice
percussion like two little bongos
in a fast mambo.

quivering inside this tiny ray
of sun struggling to sneak in.

the echo of the scent attracted
a new freedom which said, "we are
beautiful anywhere, you dig?"

my graduation speech

i think in spanish
i write in english

i want to go back to puerto rico,
but i wonder if my kink could live
in ponce, mayagüez and carolina

tengo las venas aculturadas
escribo en spanglish
abraham in español
abraham in english
tato in spanish
"taro" in english
tonto in both languages

how are you?
¿cómo estás?
i don't know if i'm coming
or si me fui ya

si me dicen barranquitas, yo reply,
"¿con qué se come eso?"
si me dicen caviar, i digo,
"a new pair of converse sneakers."

ahí supe que estoy jodío
ahí supe que estamos jodíos

english or spanish
spanish or english
spanenglish
now, dig this:

hablo lo inglés matao
hablo lo español matao
no sé leer ninguno bien

so it is, spanglish to matao
what i digo
　　　　¡ay, virgen, yo no sé hablar!

angelito's eulogy in anger

angelito is my brother
can you understand?
angelito is my brother

not that bro talk we misuse
but the real down
brother-blood-salsa   sangre de madre

angelito is my brother
dancing slow curves of misery
nodding slow-motion tunes
of alcohol dynamic soul   arrastrándose por las calles
                      con su andar de ángel-loco

standing on the usual
corner the talk of all
the affliction in the ghetto:
                      se llevó el radio
                      me escondió los cheques
                      me quitó la cartera
                      se robó el tique del ponchop

                      pero angelito lo pusieron
                      ahí mami, me entiendes

angelito was being sponsored
by soft legislators and by
the multi-million dollars
the racket is worth annually
and all of you loved the godfather
the all-time ghetto best film forever

                      me entiendes, papi
                      angelito lo tenían ahí
                      amedrentándoles las venas
                      mocosas sucias que
                      le imprentaron

a ese hermano mío
de sangre vinagrosa
húmeda de esa sangre
descalza aguada
que cambió de roja a blanca

angelito was angered
by the teacher
the preacher
the liberal
the social worker
the basketball coach
that mistreated him and
didn't let him express
his inner feelings

a angelito le hicieron un trabajo
espiritual le echaron agua
maldita le mezclaron sus buenos
pensamientos le partieron el
melodioso cantar del cucurucú
en su cantar en brujos

angelito didn't get the chance
to receive an education or to
graduate from basic english
courses   no lo querían curar
because of that once a junkie
always a junkie theory i was
taught ten years ago when
heroine had not yet invaded the
wired fences of queens. all of
a sudden drugs reach queens blvd.
and all kinds of addiction centers popped off on my block to
cure them

y tú, condenao madre y padre
a veces te digo,
por dejarte convencer

sus cabezas
por sus caprichos
de más dinero
por parar de sembrar guineos
por traernos a este
maldito sitio
donde nos ultrajaron
los bichos de varones
las tetas llenas de leche
de mi abuela
los poderosos pezones
de aquella jibarita
que se meneaba poderosamente
que me hubiese
gustado agarrarla
con mucho gusto . . .
ahora, a esa jibarita,
me la tienen
como tecata flaca
perdida en su desaliento
andando de prostituta
abriéndole las patas
al viejo palo de mapo

and the other junkies
the real junkies of the
true definition of the
word junkie (the ones
who stumped your community
with high-class hopes shaded
by lack of real attention)
they profited died fat cats
and bought their way into
heaven

nunca los oí decir ni hablar
nada sobre ellos
zánganos aguajeros
sigan tomando cervezas

sigan mirando novelas
sigan criticándose uno a otro
sigan echándole la culpa sólo
a los padres

angelito sabía todo esto
entonces él en la perdición
de su muerte está más despierto
que ustedes. angelito me dijo
todo esto. cuando yo hablo
contigo
lo único que
oigo ese el score de los mets

and the rest of you
so-called pretty looking
bad so bad dumb young
spics are sleeping underneath
the $45 price of your pants

a speech outside the jail

i'm caught in dead lock
between freedom and fear

tight as the rust
that's buried in-
side the bolted
screws of the
holland tunnel

& the erosion
of polluted waters
will dissolve me
in slow-motion
agony, as in
the process of
wrinkled veins
mellowing into
softness

i'm caught in dead lock
between freedom and fear:
inevitable companions
in the process of
thought, for freedom
as the unrestricted
improvisation feeds
the fear which is
the vanguard restriction
that molds & modifies
the original thought

perhaps those stained
by society because
of an unlawful action
upon readjusting, lose
the initial wisdom of
freedom & begin their
perceptions from fear

excommunication gossip

if it is dreams you seek
after your body is cremated
inside the grave of roofless
cemeteries.

if it is everlasting life
heaven or infinite salvation
you seek, don't cry in heaven
when you find out the lord
discriminated against minorities
if it is racism in earth you
encountered, there's a special place
for you in heaven, the official
laundromatician for virgin mary's
silk kotexes.

benditoizing the ingenious lord
who kept you secure thinking
about the sacred blessings
bestowed on them by a host

me caso en la hostia
me caso en la hostia
divina esa que trajo
muchos edificios fríos
pero el padre vivía en
la rectoría, y había mucha
agua caliente, y había mucha
agua caliente.

and the bishops
and the archbishops
and the cardinals
and the pope
slept in golden beds
i provided the good income

yes, i live on welfare
but those so-called princes

live on welfare of the people
praying contrition after contrition
and papi and myself never had anything
to say to each other . . .
(yo se lo había dicho todo al condenao
padre ese de la iglesia)

now i look at my disassociation with
papi and i blame it on you sacerdote
(todo el cariño era para mami y papi
se jodía por mí, yo nunca le presté atención)

porque tenía muchos padrastros
mentales que me alejaban de mi papá
para que yo no conociera
el porqué de sus cortejas
el porqué de sus borracheras
el porqué de los golpes malditos
porque él estaba rechazando
estas maldiciones
estas contradicciones inconscientemente

muchas basuras	keyrie eleison
muchos robos	keyrie eleison
mucho frío	keyrie eleison
sin educación	christe eleison
sin viviendas	christe eleison
sin patria	christe eleison
orando	keyrie eleison
con hambre	keyrie eleison
sin nada	keyrie eleison

and i liked the organ
cause it reminded me
of the solemn tecato notes
i would hear in the high
mass of my building . . .   a kind of motionless move
                            a kind of seeing with eyes
                    closed

                    a kind of 78-speed record
                    playing on 33

and the epistle letters
of st. paul were fabulous
the only letters
we received were dispossess
notes from the bolitero to the landlord
and everybody in between

i read a letter discharging me from school
i read a letter announcing the arrival of pedro's
    coffin from nam
i read a letter dated by mr. angel ruiz
    commissioner of the holy bible payments
    claiming my mother's favorite passage
    from her rented holy bible
i read a letter in which installment payments
    were after our family
i read a letter to subpoena my younger
    brother to court because he stole one
    lousy egg from the next door neighbor
    who had stolen it in la marketa

OREMUS

        may the sentiments
        of the people rise
        and become espiritistas
        to take care of our religious
        necessities . . .
        y echar brujos de fufú y
        espíritus malos a los que
        nos tratan como naborías
        y esclavos . . .
        and sentence them to hang
        desnudos tres días en orchard
        beach, pa que yemayá les saque
        sus maldades

subway song

strange women come down subway stairs
walking under realism, walking inside
the concrete streets.

the subway fan spreads
everybody's breath around,
people reading newspapers
not respecting each other
a long welfare turnstile of faces
seeking half-minute stardom on token ads
reminding them of what they should be
        the virginia slim liberated woman
        walking the winchester man.

how far? really how far?
leaving my innocence on cold stoops,
why is america confused?
why does she adapt foreign modes
to escape her present reality?
why am i left alone as if i were
a token outside a telephone booth?

slowly beginning to hate the make-up girl
a certain nausea . . . diarrhea
faces not integrating, and me, the between
of silent streets in nocturne caves
digging deep in faithful sleep i sing:

        nobody goes to east harlem in the morning
        nobody goes to the south bronx in the morning
        east harlem receives the subway with a sad face
        nobody wants to see beauty in the morning
        and the building on an empty lot disappears
        in the darkness of the sunny day.

my eyes are closed
my eyes are opened to see the dark world
inside the above of my eyelids.

    i found the happy spirits
        protecting me
        singing to me
        goofing with me.

something i heard

on the streets of san juan
muñoz marín stands on top
of an empty milk box
and brings his land, liberty,
bread message to a people
robbed of their existence.
napoleón's father attentively
listened as muñoz said, "independence is just around the
corner."

napoleón's father took it
literally, he went around
the corner and found a donkey
tied up to a pole.

against muñoz pamphleteering

and i looked into the dawn
inside the bread of land and liberty
to find a hollow sepulcher of words
words that i admired from my mother's eyes
words that i also imbedded as my dreams.

now i awake to find that the underneath
of your beautiful poetry pamphleteering
against the mob of stars took me nowhere
muñoz, took me nowhere, muñoz, nowhere
where i see myself inside a triangle
of contradictions with no firm bridges
to make love to those stars.

inside my ghetto i learned to understand
your short range visions of where you led us,
across the oceans where i talk about myself
in foreign languages, across where i reach
to lament finding myself re-seasoning my
coffee beans.

your sense of
stars landed me in
north temperate uprooted zone.

the last song of neruda

tell me where the vest pocket park
poverty of america is found and i shall
expose the universal suffering
every decent man strives to
eradicate:

    inside i transform my shadow
    into a puddle of water
    in a crowded street

    from there i shall rejoice
    the pains of those who step on me

    the beggar steps on me
    carries a piece of my soul
    to a deserted street
    along the way the penetrable
    hole in his shoe makes me feel
    calloused flesh hardened by all
    those suffering steps

    he takes me to the bowery
    the house of moth smell
    the disinfectant warehouse
    where coats are stored during
    summer, but here, in here,
    beggars store themselves every day
    the accumulation of rare dirt
    assembling to soil the concrete earth

    inside this assembly i shall declare
    that my poetry bleeded from prostatic
    cancer, and in exposing society's cancer
    i found the illumination of my thoughts,
    pero aun, the fallen are the purest of all

let my soul rest here on the bowery
let me create with the rarest earth

my original puddle was drained by the sun
but in my life the sun of
military fires ashed my last thoughts.

fighting

ceased to be physical
when i realized my natural
potential for dealing with
institutions on their own
word and logic turf,

ceased to be physical
as I realized
that Alvin Ailey makes
me appreciate the
modern
dance form which i
applauded because i
understood

ceased to be physical when
the power of my uneducated
prose elicited respect at a job
interview at livingston college

ceased to be physical
when i decided to stop downgrading
myself as i fused my
energies to create, to strive,
        to extend myself onto
                the largest horizon

then fighting became a constant
manifestation of my mind and my
body announcing the claim that
all of us are creative cocos

Loisaida Streets: Latinas Sing

virginity

lamentable for your many falls

i only wish, in love,
your virginity was lost,
love . . . lost . . . beautiful!

lamentable for your many falls

the ideal is to lose it young, away
from home, keeping it a secret,
feeling the passion, the look,
especially if both were virgins

lamentable for your many falls

virginity . . . thirteen . . . too old.

a message to our unwed women

tears
     dri
          p   quietly   cutting your
                                      face temporarily
eyes   SWOLLEN   NOSE a long voyage of
                                           sufrimiento

tears roll d
          o
          w
          n . . .   and you cry so deep   ly
                                so hurt

about to give birth and the lover refuses
                    and your father accuses
                    and your friends
                              con esa mirada

tears
     dri
     p   quietly   in the dark room
                                      you sleep

tears are there
in the morning   that morning
                        when you walked down
                        the tenements up
                        the streets to la bodega

"adiós, ¿y cuándo
te casastes?"
                        and they gave you
                        the half mirada
                        and you bit the tears
                        from showing up

you walked knowing   eyes were talking
                       eyes were following
                       eyes were criticizing

"look at . . .
she was such a good girl!"
as if your life had stopped
as if you dropped an atom bomb
as if you had to walk in shame
as if
as if
as if

tears suddenly stopped
in the most majestic manner
that pleased only yourself
you quietly said:
>   "i am now a true woman
>   my child will not be called
>   illegitimate
>   this act was done with love
>   with passion
>   my feelings cannot be planned
>   i will not let their innocence
>   affect me
>   i will have him, coño,
>   because i want him
>   because i feel this breast
>   of life consoling
>   my hurt, sharing my grief,
>   if anybody does
>   not accept it
>   que se vayan pal . . . me entienden
>   pal . . . lo oyen
>   pal . . . me escuchan."

the sun radiated
the streets became alive
"to give birth **A LA RAZA**
is the ultimate that i can
ever give."

a sensitive bolero in transformation
(*for anne sexton*)

se   no
se   no
                              breast
                              breast

se   sensual
no   se
suspiro
                              breast
                              hard
                              duro
                              mistreated
                              maltratado
                              manoseado

seno
seno no se . . .   han abierto
                              se están
                              desarrollando
                              buscando
                              la fuerza
                              dios mío
                              la fuerza
                              de crear
                              de despojar   ¡leche!   ¡leche!

el jugo that juices   the softest flow
                              inside the veins
                              of my heart—my
                              definition of
                              brownness

seno
                              my secluded eyes
                              the darkest shade
                              of tan the sun
                              gives me

seno encarcelado

solamente el sol
me ha tratado suavemente,
constantemente . . . solamente el sol me ha dado
energía

seno suave

breast caliente
creates all the
modos   all the
feelings of my colors

seno   my third and fourth eyes

my longing is the   meñique
anular
del corazón
índice
pulgar
fingers of a hand
treat my breasts as sculptures
choreographing the mental and
spiritual ballet that would
make his lips and then his
body define me in my barest
nudity to make the contact
of harvesting flowless energy
in space

seno   sensual
seno   orgánico

why then
do you treat them
just as breasts?

the song of an oppressor

simplemente maría
simplemente maría
maría maría

>>Doña Eusebia's knees were eliminated
>>simple
>>her head an army boot upside down
>>mente
>>her tongue was out from exhaustion
>>maría

they took advantage
>simple
english was foreign to you
>mente
era el goofer del landlord de nuestras vidas
>maría

>>the tv tube
>>simple
>>whose jeringuillas
>>mente
>>made us addicted de la mente
>>maría

how was it done?   simplemente maría

the exploiter rang the cash
>simple
registered on a plane
>mente
to new york or his cadillac in queens
>maría

>>in my anger i replied
>>mami mami
>>looking at dead novelas

about natacha
about renzo the gypsy
feeling sorry about
the poor maid
feeling sorry about
the way she's treated
like a dog
like a slave
mami mami
stop saying
ay benditos and lamentos
why?
because in real life,
natacha is you eres tú eres tú eres tú

simplemente maría
simplemente maría
maría maría

i turned off the tv and said:
madre madre madre mía
always suffering at the knees
of your children. playing
on broadway off off broadway
every day, far from movies
theatres luxury hotels
under the direct supervision
of the landlords of our lives
who yell, "TRABAJO CHIPE
PISS WORK UN CHAVO POR
CADA VEINTE TRAJES."

madre madre madre mía
living like a whore
to buy legal aid
from storefront lawyers
who tell your son
to plead guilty

madre madre madre mía
those crystallized dreams about
america cars homes fortunes
were buried inside the needle
of the singer machine

s-i-m-p-l-e-m-e-n-t-e-m-a-r-í-a
s-i-m-p-l-e-m-e-n-t-e-m-a-r-í-a

mami, you sit so calmly
looking at your novelas
looking at your children
caring so much for them
your love as silent as the lead
writing on paper
                as natural as the falling
                autumn leaves
                as eternal as the rising moon
                the setting sun

mami, tears of sacrifice sanctify
your delicate face, valley of tears
in your heart
mami, i love you
this spirit of love gives me rancor
and hatred, and i react to the song
simplemente maría. but my anger,
my hate
is based on love, ultimate love of you!

mami, you are my epitome
                but i shall be your sword

simplemente maría
simplemente maría
maría   maría

titi teita and the taxi driver

mire, señor, mis familiares no han venido,
estoy perdida en el aeropuerto,
pero, yo sé la dirección, la calle
watel estrí

no se apure, señora, yo la llevaré
deme 50 pesos.

la tecata

sighs in front of garbage:
slimy mucous saliva engages
into vowels of overdosed movements
(the slow passivity of eyes closing)
begins output of expressive energy,
horns and flutes coming out into
the windows playing her out into
making her una madama scratching
hair in slow motion tecato scars
arranging herself to be hidden
inside the basement out of touch
with the horns improvising on her
without coming out to guide her.

the suffering of ruth santiago sánchez

oh, but my days are spent
in spiritual anger hearing
the crusty cries of ghetto
hearts living underground

despite that fact that yesterday
humanless landlords brought
about housing destruction and today
i'm trying to preserve
eighteenth-century abandoned
structures wearing the weight of so many
immigrants.

the immigrants are still coming
but the buildings are
speculated to exclude people.

soledad

people talk about loneliness

is only sexual companionship
that's soon forgotten

people talk about solitude

beneath its seven layers
nobody can talk about solitude

and soledad

well, there is no english
translation

nightcap

a retrieve back into
personal. usually no
holes barred. compatibility.
he wants.   she needs.
he needs.   she wants.

the games of love turned
romantic pinches.
the moon does not walk,
she does not dare to give out
a bad wave.

palm tree in spanglish figurines

slowly, as in son montuno,
she erases frustrated tears
from face to hand . . . she dances . . .

natural coconut rhythms
swaying soul essences
and latino salsa all
intertwine within her

ocean eyes followed
her bolero-slow sensual movements
in cha-cha turned sharp curves,
a mysterious cult
inside the feelings of
ancestral bomba and plena

the maunabo indian emerged from her hips

piñones was her face setting

eyes looking for turtle eggs
mouth tasting cangrejos
in madrugada's solemnity

ocean eyes followed
interacting   within
screaming   above
searching   underneath
her latin dance
her escape from the
tear that collapsed
into daylight's hands
creating happiness

the congas mujer

a new woman was born!
her outstretched hands
carried the echoes
of madness to far away ears
oppression and love merged
pain and happiness fused
cuchifritos and books raped each other
america the beautiful woman
also was a prostitute in disguise
all prostitutes became mary magdalenes
the complete change
the ultimate despojo of oppression released
machismo and respect confronted each other
the sound has been ignited!
the motor running at great speed!
hand-powered attitudes driving powerfully!
driving onto the physical self!
destroying it, constructing . . .
a new woman! a new woman . . .
she shouted, and danced, and cried openly
without any hesitation
without any fear
making everyone deal with her
a new woman! a new woman!
beyond the criticism of the people
to the true self
the self that cried independence!
the self that analyzed calling major surgery!
the self that looked at man admiringly, not possessively
the self that is the self that is the self that is

El Arrabal: Nuevo Rumbón

the new rumbón

congas   congas   congas
congas   congas   congas

desperate hands need a fix from
the healthy skin of the congas
congas the biggest threat to heroin
congas make junkies hands healthier

las venas se curan ligero
con las congas conguito congas
congueros salsa de guarapo
melao azucarero

congas on summer months
take the place of the winter
fire that the wino congregation
seeks, the fire . . .

que calienta los tecatos muertos de
frío en el seno de un verano

congas gather around

con un rumboncito caliente . . .
y ahí vienen los morenos
a gozar con sus flautas y su soul jazz

congas   congas
tecata's milk gets warmed
broken veins leave misery
hypodermic needles melt
from the voodoo curse
of the conga madness

the congas clean the gasses
in the air, the congas burn out
everything not natural to our people

congas strong cuchifrito juice
giving air condition to faces
unmolested by the winds and the
hot jungles of loisaida streets
chévere, rumbones, me afectó
me afectó, me afectó, me afectó

chévere   rumbones   me afectó.

felipe luciano i miss you in africa

hey you black smooth stallion!
hey you black smooth stallion!
hey you black smooth stallion!
hey you reverberator of present definitions!
hey you pretty niggerito whom i have seen
since blackness penetrated the pores of my emotions!
hey you suntanned rainbow-skinned
ghetto preacher definitor
of new negritos:

     i love missing you in africa with me,
     to hear your hands clapping soulfully
     spanglispan spanglispan spanglispan
     phrases that make me think:
     i love missing you in africa!

     am reacting subtly to africa,
     i wish you were here with me, hermano,
     to make beauty with you, felipe,
     attending to the matters of Black Brazil
     creating definitions that redefine
     blackness again and again and all over again.
     god damn it, felipe!
     i love missing you in africa with me,
     nurturing my senses broader and broader, brother,
     making definitions out of eye scratch:
     "princely," "aristocratic," "gods"
     nothing but unifying statements.

     i love missing you in africa.
     africa misses the drums of your thoughts,
     she waits to give you citizenships:
     Oba of el Barrio
     Otun of Salsa
     she waits for you singing:
     what was made by slavery
     impossible,

has been made by africa
wonderfully possible!
to esteem thorns
of our major roots

were	luba	mi	ce		
were	luba	mi	ce		
were	luba	mi	ce		
ohun	ti	aro	e	ko	ce	ce

the africa in pedro morejón

slowly descending, as if from the clouds above,
thinking of africa, i find myself enthralled!
rhythmic africanism swell and dwell inside
the fingers of my cuban mambo eyes.

the african rhythms i hear are native, native
from my cuban land, it is as if my guaguancó
was shipped to àfrica, when it was the other
way around, but nevertheless all my colors are the same.

i hear the merengue in french haiti
and in dominican blood,
and the guaracha in yoruba,
and the mambo sounds inside the plena
so close to what i really understand,
sometimes i think
that cuba is africa,
or that i am in cuba and africa at the
same time, sometimes i think africa
is all of us in music,
musically rooted way way back
before any other language.

yes, we preserved what was originally african,
or have we expanded it? i wonder if we have
committed the sin of blending? but i also hear
that AFRICANS love electric guitars clearly misunderstanding they are the root,
or is it me who is primitive?
damn it, it is complicated.

i had a dream that i was in africa,
it took me a long time
to find the gods inside
so many moslems and christians,
but when i did, they were the origin of everything!
then i discovered bigger things,

the american dollar symbol,
that's african;
the british sense of royalty, that's african;
the colors in catholic celebrations,
that's african; and . . .
ultimate . . . listen here . . . closer . . .
come on . . . closer . . . sshhhhhh . . .
two whites can never make a black . . .
two whites can never make a black . . .
two whites can never make a black . . .
but two blacks, give them
time can . . . make mulatto . . .
can make brown . . . can make blends . . .
and ultimately . . . can make white.

óyeme consorte, pero no repita esto,
porque si me coge el klu klux klan
me caen encima con un alemán
me esparrachan con una swastika
y me cortan la cabeza. pero, es verdad:
dos blancos no pueden hacer un prieto.

i went to africa and all of it seemed cuban,
i met a cuban and all of him was african,

this high-priest, pedro, telling me all of this
in front of an abandoned building.

savorings, from piñones to loíza

to combine the smell of tropical
plaintain roots   sofritoed
into tasty crispy platanustres
after savoring a soft mofongo
with pork rind pieces, before
you cooked them into an escabeche
peppered with garlic tostones
at three o'clock in a piñones sunday afternoon, after your body cremated itself dancing the night, madrugando
in san juan beaches, walking over
a rooster's cucu rucu and pregonero's
offering of wrapped-up alcapurrias
fried in summer sun . . .
hold yourself strong
ahead is the Ancón, the crossing to loíza . . .
you have entered the underneath
of plena, mi hermano,
steady rhythms that constantly don't change
steady rhythms that constantly don't change
tru cu tú   tru cu tú
tru cu tú   tru cu tú
tu   tu   tu

el moreno puertorriqueño
(*a three-way warning poem*)

qué voy a ser yo como moreno
puertorriqueño. preguntar
¿dónde está mi igualdad?
viendo novelas sobre morenos
esclavos, sin poder ver un
moreno en la pantalla. la
negra dorotea, el nené mingo,
papá cortijo, la morenita to-
masa, todos son blancos dis-
frazados, haciendo papeles sin
vida, haciéndose burla de mi
presencia. tratando de asimilar
mi color negroide para mejorar
la raza, ¿qué pienso yo?
¿qué pensarán mis compañeros?
les pregunto yo, ¿soy yo igual
soy yo todavía esclavo?

ñam ñam yo no soy
de la masucamba
ñam ñam yo no soy
de la masucamba

ay baramba bamba
suma acaba
quimbombo de salsa
la rumba matamba
ñam ñam yo no soy
de la masucamba
papiri pata pata
loíza musaraña
bembón ay no canta
el cañonero es de acero
las puertas arrebatan
changó cambió color
es de la raza cumbamba
si no me quieres mi compay
te echaré flores
sin abundancia

poem negroide

palabras de Palés Matos

summer wait

with the thought of
seven long months ahead i
await to see
your green . . .
the many jam sessions
i took in, would they
give me enough winter
warmth? within leafless
trunk trees timidly towering
over my solitude, i await
your return, humming to the tunes
of dry leaves
slowly scratching cemented sentiments
making maraca-sound noises.

tumbao

(*for eddie conde*)

tumbao is the spiritual rhythm of the nod
tumbao is the spiritual gathering of the congas
tumbao and tumbao met . . .

1.

tucutú pacutú   tucutú pacutú
tucutú pacutú   tucutú pacutú

aguacero de mayo que va a caer
aguacero de mayo que va a caer

ya estoy cansado de llorar
y estoy llorando
. . . llora como llore . . .
y estoy llorando
con la lengua afuera

2.

warm the fiery explosions
of hunger
come on cuchifrito juice
juana pena cries
boone's farm apple juice
juana pena dances
she shows slow curves
deep birth moans
a dead stomach that aches

3.

conguero
espíritu coroso
llamamba quimbembe
sin bajo
un hueco en el corazón
conguero . . . sonero
prisionero del parque arrabal

conguero
pito que pita
yuca que llama
salsa que emprende
llanto que llora
última llamada sin fuego
tumba que la tamba
tumba que la bamba baja
que pacheco se inspira
que ismael la canta
¡oh!   y el baquiné

4.

meaning childbirth
meaning sacrament of death
        instead of baptism
meaning solitude
meaning anger . . .

5.

and the park   those ghetto parks
the living-room-kitchen
of many desperate souls
tumbao movements
street gutted salsa

6.

¡¡conguero!!
you bite frustrated
wine twistered definitions
and the winos find employment
for their wretched lives
reminiscing on the women
that left them because they
couldn't take it anymore

7.

conguero   despojero

tumbador   crazy boogie man

conguero   sonero

artista   manipulador
you can't take it aaahhh!
you can't take it aaahhh!
you can't take it aaahhh!
close your lips
expose your hands
give us your tired
your beaten your triste soledad
and sing for me . . . allá en el africa central
          hay unos negros
            que se perdieron en puerto rico
trucutú pacutú   trucutú pacutú
trucutú pacutú   trucutú pacutú

8.
cowbells from empty wine bottles
empty congas   cemented hands
all these sounds
about words
around faces
coming from tito,
hermano mío,
coño, nodding on the streets

like un tumbao

summer congas
(*pregnancy and abortion*)

from far away   i saw the congas playing
winos screamed
putas danced
soneros sang guaguancó tunes
the rest were spectators
ogling at themselves

from far away   i saw the congas playing
so hard that they were
buried in the pavement
the drummer creating sounds
from the sidewalk floor
the breeze carried them to far away ears

misunderstanding people
protested their fears
             pigeons were fed
             crap game found rhythm
             lovers made music
             system retaliated

from far away   i saw the congas playing
everyone walked to the tunes
tatatatá tutututú tucutupacutú
heroine sugar hands were exploiting
the last tune before winter oblivion

from far away   i saw the congas playing
junkies cooking
drummers now diluting . . .

congas catching cold,
uncultural weather . . .
trees received winter warmth . . .
spirits aborted a suffering

negrito, who became the winter drum
fire that reminisced those
three beautiful summer months.

from far away
and now
too cold

the salsa of bethesda fountain

the internal feelings we release
when we dance salsa
is the song of manu dibango
screaming africa
as if it were a night in el barrio
when the congas are out

the internal soul of salsa
is like don quijote de la mancha
classical because the roots are
from long ago, the symbol of cervantes writing in pain of a lost
right arm, and in society today,
the cha-cha slow dance welfare

the internal spirit of salsa
is an out-bembé on sunday afternoons
while felipe flipped his sides
of the cuban-based salsa
which is also part of africa
and a song of the Caribbean

the internal dance of salsa
is of course plena
and permit me to say these words
in afro-spanish:
la bomba y la plena puro son
de Puerto Rico que ismael es el
rey y es el juez
meaning the same as marvin gaye
singing spiritual social songs
to black awareness

a blackness in spanish
a blackness in english
mixture-met on jam sessions in central park,
there were no differences in

the sounds emerging from inside
soul-salsa is universal
meaning a rhythm of mixtures
with world-wide bases

did you say you want it stronger?
well, okay, it is a root called africa in
all of us.

haiku

shanghai   streets   of san juan
split   between   two   realities
and   one   people

orchard beach y la virgen del carmen

and latin joe made the congas mad
    the sea waves receded
    there was a tornado in the sand
    the boardwalk cracked
    the people all stopped all danced
            consciously or subconsciously

and latin joe and the congas were tripping
    the fingers named themselves
        meñique   anular   del
        corazón   índice   pulgar
        making heaven-hell sounds

    the sun sat next to the moon
    the birds stopped in mid-air

and victor quinteando was beautiful
    like cacique tunes keeping the rhythms

    the beer sold faster
    the grass was traveling at great speed
    the junkies found something
    that kept pace with their melodies
    the sounds raped all the virgins
    that were left

and ismaelito sang his father's tunes
    there was no difference
    Moti agua . . .
    Yemayá Yemayá oh! oh! oh!
    Agua que va a caer
    Agua que va a caer
    Agua que va a caer

        the rain was coming down
        but the winds stopped it
and latin joe
and latin faces
        footmarks imprinted in the sand
        were even dancing
        the congas were laid
        and reached their climax!
        tru cu tú pacutú
        tru cu tú pacutú
        tru cu tú pacutú
and nobody said it was inspired by
LA VIRGEN DEL CARMEN
coming out of the sun

canción para un parrandero

hombre sencillo   hombre sencillo
dime ¿qué regalo quieres
para la navidad?

hombre sencillo, lumpen . . .

"oye negrito, yo quiero CLARIDAD
bueno, negrito, yo creo en la Bomba para gozar

para la mujer   el hombre
para vacilar   la yerba buena, pero buena de verdad
para palés matos   el baquiné
para loíza   estar en su carnaval
para Puerto Rico   pues, para el puertorriqueño

tú ves, negrito, yo no pido más
tú ves, negrito, yo no pido más
vamos para la esquina a poner a los pobres
a gozar por un ratito nada más / a gozar por
un ratito nada más / a gozar por un ratito nada más /
a gozar para estar en paz / a gozar por un ratito
corto que tenemos y después . . . / tú sabes
lo que trajo el barco / no hay que decir más nada".

la música jíbara

derramando décimas con lágrimas
suplicándole a su mano "paciencia"
intrigando coordinación adentro del ojo
el cantor de las montañas sacaba el lo

pensando en el café perfumante
oliéndolo en montañas y arrabales
tirando la pava hacia la sombra
que congaba las tetas de cayey salía el le

y jorge brandon nos dice: "el jíbaro puertorriqueño
que siente amor por su tierra, quiere vivir en la sierra,
y ser de su casa dueño, vivir en la hamaca un sueño,
soñar con su patria chica, beber ron de caña rica,
jugarle todo a su gallo, robarse una hembra a caballo,
y morir como mojica". de jorge brandon salía el lai

lo   le   lo   lai   lo   le   lo   lai . . .

un minuto adentro de un segundo
sale la guitarra con su tiempo
infinito de perfección, con su
tiempo infinito de una canción.

¡oh! le vino en una inspiración, tal vez.
pero qué mucho camello paseando por
soles puertorriqueños ardientes.

doña cisa y su anafre

doña cisa estaba adentro la media madrugada
la noche entera se reflejaba en la luna
al son del verano, cogiendo el resfriado
que brinda el aire reumático, que camina en la pobreza.

[García Lorca]

la luna bailaba muy suave, buscando su reflexión
en la tierra, buscando un alma o un instante
merecido a compararse con su belleza.

analfabeteando entre sílabas, la luna así decía:
   "cilusana   luanasa   *[palabras de sonido articulane]*
   lusacina   lunacisa
   luna   cisa."
y también encontró el anafre, el instante
merecido y el alma entusiasmada.

parándose en un instante, transformada en dulce
voz de melodía, la luna así decía:

   "ese ruido calentón, que escurre bacalaítos
   hacía de Harina oro, doña cisa vende
   bacalao para comprar pegao cuando el rico   *[to carract (arroz)]*
   lo bota entregándoselo a los gatos".

   'Bacalaítos',   entre su rugosa piel-dignidad.

   'Bacalaítos',   gritaba ella, con ese entusiasmo
                    con ese querer.

   'Bacalaítos',   sus ojos oprimían la leña
                    le daba fuerza al anafre
                    que vivió de lujo en el pasado   *[(lloraba unido).]*
                    que vive de luto en el presente.   *[(matado, quemado)]*

   'Bacalaítos',   guardaba en su vejez una fierosa
                    juventud, dándole estímulo a calles
                    llenas de tristeza.

'Bacalaítos',   hechos con el sabor de manos
mezclando alrededor alrededor
y yo luna bailando a las tres
de la mañana, ¡oh, conocí
las nubes para disfrutar el buen
pensamiento a solas de mi soledad!"

doña cisa cantaba al son de la noche
perfumándola lentamente suavemente
dándole sabor al aire reumático
creando sin vanidad al nuevo jíbaro
que ponía firmes pies en el seno de
américa quemando ritmos africanos y
mitos indígenas.

      "guarden sus chavitos prietos",
gritaba doña cisa,
      "guarden sus chavitos prietos",
gritaban sus dedos borinqueños
mientras mordían las llamas del fuego
que quemaban esa noche loisaideña
escogiendo el camino

      ni regular
      ni suave
      ni cósmico
pero el camino-carrito-cultural
del pensamiento típico.

doña cisa no refunfuñaba, no maldecía
el anafre gritaba de alegría cuando
el rasca rasca rasca que rasca
dientes jibaritos, chupándose las bocas
mordiéndose los dedos del sabor olor
bacalaítos fritos color oro
dignidad.

      el sol salió besando a la luna
anafreándola con amor.

santa bárbara

Tema africano. santería

entramos, todo está preparado
la música de changó era la luz del día.

entramos,   a la fiesta espiritual
          a lo rojo
          a lo santa bárbara.

baila   baila   dale vueltas
indios se levantan de su genocidio
negros se despiertan en sus espíritus
voces de las velas empiezan a hacer
dibujos espirituales en mis ojos.

hay algo, sí, sí, hay algo, algo
el vino está preparado, los cigarros se encienden   _rito_
los santos se levantan a hacer fiesta
todo está preparado.

y martina
y el ángel de la casa
se transforma en un indio burgués
y la señora de la casa está vestida de blanco, _puerta, promesa_ _abstención_
rojo previene en nuestras vidas.

despojos   algunos suaves   _sale el espíritu_
          algunos fuertes
          algunos incrédulos

despojos en guayama _(pueblo afrocaribeño)_
y la gente se levanta
esperando si santa bárbara
desciende de su trono
y cambia color a lo
negro coroso negroide.

dolores me vio sentirme incrédulo
yo no creía, no, no, yo no creía
pero había algo, y dolores se despojó
como una princesa taína, su cuerpo desnudo
con esa fuerza, dios mío, con esa fuerza,
esa fuerza, esa fuerza, esa fuerza que
>   rompe la rapidez del viento
>   y me hace sentir sudor
>   y me hace escupir lágrimas
>   alborotadas.

cogí un suspiro, paré de respirar
las venas se me querían salir,
dolores y martina se inspiraban,
me acosté al lado de una pared sobre
la puerta, cerré los ojos,
los abrí un poquito
las luces se veían pequeñas
empecé a moverme, moverme, moverme,
no sé por qué, ahí supe que me iban
a despojar, me concentré, levanté las manos . . . y me fui

>   bailé como guarionex
>   recité como juan borias
>   canté como ismael

alguien real maravilloso
me tocó mi íntimo ser
creo que fue ELLA
extendiéndose las manos.

coreografía

Aída . . . traje blanco . . . escena verde . . . luz amarilla

plenea
canta rumba en rumbón
suave las caderas
fuerte el coro del son
mantiene congas despiertas
se mueve con la brisa del sol

plenea
por las calles de loíza
del fanguito en el bronx

plenea rumbas de loíza
en el parque central

Aída baila majestad
se ve un barco de negros
ofreciendo ayuda a las
reglas de caridad . . .
Aída baila entre pellejos
del conga cuero
collares a muchos colores . . .
Aída su voz sonriente
le hace cariño al sol

por allí viene la noche,
¡Aída cantaba oh Aída cantaba!
se arropaba en blanco vestuario
las congas están calientes
las congas están calientes
se inspiró . . . salió yemayá
congueros calentando
al son del son

¡Aída cantaba oh Aída cantaba!
sus mejillas acariciaban la noche
sus manos eran indios de asia
un clavito rojo en su bello cabello
. . . yemayá el coro coro o yemayá
manos en cinturas
manos en pulseras
manos en collares
manos expresivas
todo el mundo en collares

Iván maraqueaba fuerte
Iván maraqueaba protectivo
maracas racas racas
impulsaban a Aída
inspiraban a Aída
exaltaban a Aída
su madre rezaba
al punto más alto
preservando bombas

acariciando plenas
soneando improvisaciones negroides
todo el mundo . . . a cantar
a llorar
a despojar
a reír
a encontrar lo que es vivir

II

Aída . . . traje colorado . . . escena edificios . . . luz amarilla

era viernes, Aída recorría
en el tren gusano
abastecido de miedo miedo
su cara asustada que
alguien la atracaría

Aída miraba la noche
en su corrida por calle simpson,
caras admiraban Aída:
ese rojo orgulloso de su andar
pero la luna estaba triste
escupiendo pedazos de nubes
triste vomitando el sol medio dormido
"¡qué horrorosa noche!"
"¡qué horrorosa noche!"
Aída decía

en la esquina, el vinillo ardiente
prostitutas-hermanas vivían la soledad
dentro de sus siete pellejos
Aída . . . negra noche
Aída . . . negra angustia

los celos de él
los celos vengativos
querían encarcelar su belleza
en control supremo
esas peleas que inspiraban Aída
a cantar la opresión de la bomba
en las caras dolorosas en nuestros hermanos:
los que cometen el delito de la aguja
por el tren de satisfacción

adentro de la sociedad
más baja más hundida
por esas calles de simpson
por esas calles de fox
y él se apareció de momento

sin hablar le entregó en las frases
de sus mejillas cortadas
por el frío calentoso
de una navaja que acariciaba
su bella cara y le sobaba la
sangre derramada en la cutis
infierno de la calle

Aída, ya flaca, despojada
en un lamento dolor
subía escaleras
llamando súplicas negroides
nadie la entendía y la sangre
roja de su tierna cara le corría
a su rojo traje —el ave de
siete muertos en ruedas murmullaban
al río ¡oh la negra sonera
sufriendo boleros pálidos y hondos
qué dolor, qué angustia!

sus manos en pulseras de sangre
se maraqueaban como un ala de
hoja muerta
sus mejillas aclimaban al negrindio
sus ojos miraban hasta el cielo
sin estrellas hasta el cielo de sucio
nadie presente
sola
qué extremo, ¿verdad?
qué extremo, ¿verdad?

y él no corrió
le gustó por un
diablo momento
verla sufrir   sin cantar
                 sin cantar
"eres mía   mía
me cantarás sólo a mí
                 o
no le cantarás a nadie".

III

Aída . . . traje marrón . . . escena blanca . . . luz amarilla

en la cama abortada
adentro del dolor

Aída gritaba gritaba sufriendo
muerte en esa cama
muerte en esa cama
muchos negros le rezaban
a su vida y no a su muerte
lloraban el dolor interno
se inspiraban en la venganza
su madre se pretendía fuerte
en preparación en preparación
recogiendo matas y hierbas
buscando a santeras y espiritistas
    "Dios, no me la dejes sufrir
    Dios, no la dejes sufrir
    con la muerte. Dios, no me
    desengañes, no me abandones.
    Dios piadoso, por favor te
    ruego, te ofrezco este hábito,
    te doy mi alma entera. ¡Oh!
    Dios potente me acuesto en tu
    servidumbre, te doy esta promesa,
    no me lleves la hija mía".

en la noche su espíritu se paró
sufriendo de dolor
recordando aquel momento
de Aída en inspiración
la vimos volando en su traje blanco
en su traje blanco de festejo
y voló del dolor y voló del dolor
yemayá las potencias de las súplicas
del mar le limpiaban con su virgen
caridad, las aguas buenas del morir
vivir le apoyó por su espíritu limpio,
le dio nuevamente su pelea

su espíritu le volvió a su cuerpo
en ese momento   momento tenso
con tantos ojos   que no eran ingratos

abrió los ojos   abrió los ojos
llamando a todos un fuerte abrazo
       "con Dios todos, sin Dios nada
       volveré a captar   volveré a cantar
       volveré a bailar   y perdón
       le doy a mi fiel amado
       que me comprenda
       que vi en su acto de violencia
       un acto de amor".

el sonero mayor

el hombre hablaba
se inspiraba desde
cárceles hoteles
extraños países

        "déjenme irme que es
        muy tarde ya"

un hit disco detrás del otro

        "para lo que tú le da"

cinco bolsitas de coca
porque estaba

        "en la triste soledad
        de mi celda yo compuse
        esta canción para ti"

parrandeaba las calles
de loíza, de la tapia
hablando de los espíritus y

        "negros carabalí que
        con su ritmo i na rará
        bailan así y dicen así"

y que quizás se habían perdido
en puerto rico, y siempre
por todo puerto rico
por el fanguito del south bronx
por las calles llenas de pobres
por todos los social clubs
se oía:

        SU VOZ ILUMINOSA
        EL SONERO MAYOR
        EL TEORÉTICO DE NUESTRAS VIDAS

él me dio, y le da
a muchos condenados en la tierra
su único momento
de placer y de alegría

"dime por qué me abandonaste
no me atormentes, amor, no me
mates, ten compasión dime
por qué"

y yo estaba pensando cuál era
la razón que él decía

"en este mundo si uno no se
alaba no hay quien lo alabe"

y ese hombre cuya voz enérgica
y poderosa le daban

"para lo que tú le das
tú le das tú le das
tú le das tú le das
palo, puño y bofetá"

nosotros bailábamos
sus cantos alumbraban,
en todos bembés
sus ídolos lo imitaban
había algo positivo
en su belleza
ismael y su swing maravilloso
me entiendes

"juan josé, pasé por tu
casa y te llamé. Juan
josé como no me oístes
te pité"

pero creo que había un vacío
en su alma, a veces oíamos
sus canciones pero no lo que
él decía, solamente mi hermano
pablo y todos los compañeros
de la soledad y la ironía:

los de las cárceles . . . los de fort worth . . . los de lex.ky . . .
los de la 110 . . . los de la castro viña . . . los del barrio obrero . . .
los de martín peña . . . los de puerta de tierra . . .
los lumpen pobres de la tierra

veían a ismael como una luz
poderosa en nuestras vidas

en orchard beach
conocí a su hijo ismaelito
y cantaba   igual
y soneaba   igual
y se movía   igual
                        igual que
                        su padrecito

y pensé.

declamación

¡Oh! . . . don Jorge . . . JORGE BRANDON.
yo a ti, te veo . . . en mis nubes,
quebrando el hilo de la imaginación
qué de prenda, diamante . . . ilumina la vejez
en el día madrugante

¡Oh! . . . don Jorge . . . JORGE BRANDON.
pan que alimenta   sin pesares . . .
canción del muerto vivo . . . llanto de los que
lloran . . . gritando . . . sol de los pobres que luchan
ídolo de los héroes de patria
transformación a cualquier sufrimiento
pensador de todos . . . orador de nadie

¡Oh! . . . don Jorge . . . JORGE BRANDON
te quiero tal como nadie nunca to ha querido
eres como la canción de Rafael Hernández
como la palabra inspiradora de Pedro Albizu
el concepto del vocablo PATRIA que Luis Muñoz
le dio a los carreteros.

¡Oh! . . . don Jorge . . . JORGE BRANDON.
padre espiritual de todos ellos,
en tu poesía encomiendo mi madre,
mis hijos, mi patria, mi abuela . . .
el pan nuestro de cada día dánoslo hoy
y perdónanos nuestras deudas porque
tus décimas son lágrimas
tu vida es muerte en espíritu
tu espíritu es aliento al que te encuentra
tu fama es el futuro . . . cuando ánimas
que conozcan grandeza, se cuelan a estudiar
la prosa de un santo

¡Oh! . . . don Jorge . . . JORGE BRANDON.
te toqué como Jesús fue tocado
por Verónica y sentí las palabras
poderosas del autor profeta
de las aguas santas.

¡Oh! . . . don Jorge . . . JORGE BRANDON.
¿en qué sitio apropiado
te escribo yo estas lágrimas?
donde el grito es de victoria
aquí en la arena del madison square garden
adentro, el luchador pedro morales
es un ídolo del pobre que lo acoge
y lo alienta en el desengaño romántico
de ganar entre los países más grandes
      entre las piedras olvidadas
      entre el mar profundo de bellezas
      entre el fervor del despojo de llamas

¡Oh! . . . don Jorge . . . JORGE BRANDON.
y ganó una ilusión, pedro morales
¡pero ganó un grito eterno!
¡un llanto admirable!
¡un suspiro de fuerza!
qué . . . Dios mío, ¡Dios mío!
se quedaba . . . nunca fue rechazado
ni vencido . . .
¡los de abajo! ¡Oh, los de abajo!
desde allí escribe Brandon
y ese grito espiritual-poeta
nunca será reemplazado
en américa dirán,
"era el GRITO más alto".

¡Oh! . . . don Jorge . . . JORGE BRANDON.
a veces me pierdo entre brujos que hacen mal . . .
me desánimo entre el bien que no progresa . . .

me agito con almas que no creen en paz . . .
pero te toqué, . . . al tocarte mis hijos te tocarán, . . .
las frases del ánimo en tu vejez, en tu experiencia
te piden el beso, . . .

      el beso que no tiene otro igual
      el beso Padre de Borinquen
      el beso Madre-Corazón
      el beso de . . . don Jorge . . . JORGE BRANDON.

EnClave

Feelings of One

jorge brandon

poetry is an outcry, love, affection,
a sentiment, a feeling, an attitude,
a song.

it is internal gut expressing intimate
thoughts upon a moment's experience.

poetry is the incessant beauty called
a person by an action that takes form.

the smell of sand in water digging moon
the loving smile.

poetry is the mountain, the recital,
the reaction, the desire, to feel
right in wrong, to taste bitter
memory, to praise death, to mourn,
to call.

poetry, oh, poetry:

beautiful novels in short lived prose.

long live your concise aristocracy!

long live your detailed concrete forms!

long live the people who espouse you!

long live sentiments of love!

long live unending desires, on and on
forever on:

poetry poetry

a poeta called

the soul!

jesús papote

It was untouched energy that reached
the shakings of his embryonic testicles
he moved eyes closed body crouched face
inside her body nobody knew his identity
not even his name he laid inside casket
corpse brethren woman strung out deep
cornered jungle streets eyes closed body
crouched face tucked pregnant belly salivating umbilical cord peddling multi-
cut heroin sub-ghetto fortress chanting
early winter 25 degree cold-frío shivering
lacked attention lacked warmth born-to-be
embryo asphyxiated 25 dollars powers penetrating veins venas veins venas pouring
rivers pouring up mountain muscles brain's
tributaries.

She allowed herself to be touched old men
seeking last minute enjoyment thrills
social security military retirement pensions
on the woman about to give birth body running
down 13th Street looking desperately for the
fix the fix hope-esperanza fix satisfaction
she tripped pained herself bleeding internally
the water bag had broken she did not care her
jugular veins were asking for attention to be
fed intravenously that was her priority to
satisfy her veins pinpointed needle metal rape
open pores scar-burnt hands.

She reached 1980 lower east side's 9th street going
up down empty cellars abandoned building
drug hideouts sad desperation christmas eve
thighs scratching up down abandoned lot she
met the fix la cura the fix la cura cura cura
she escaped stars relaxation she dreamt opium
drug re-leaving her into fantasy world beyond

universe still body mind ecstasy diluted chem-
icals soothing pain in brain she felt no body
no-motion-body knocked by powerful earthly drug
heroin she wanted heroin yes yes she wished
she loved heroin slow motion ejaculations
exploding nervous system open-preyed flesh human
body not feeling dry winter air christmas eve
nochebuena 12 o'clock tranquility night of peace
no mangers night of hope heroin reaching embryo
about-to-be-born little child silent night feeding
tubes struggling to survive being born to die
pneumonia choking or overdosed body 12 o'clock
abandoned lot dying fire all by himself alone:

He was born star of peace church bells
he was born busting out loud cry church bells
he was born son grand son great grand son
he was born generations america puerto rico
he was born europe africa 7 generations before
he was born latest legacy family tree inheritor
he was born he was born 20th century
urban story greatest told abandonment
concrete land new york city story of stories
contemporary poets felt the spirit in the air
those who searched for lost souls new prophecies
celebrating jesus christ one thousand nine hundred and eighty times seeking christ spirit
ritual midnight mass family dinners children
fast asleep santa claus is coming silent night
holy night he pushed an echo into death's eulogy
one speech one experience one smell one feeling
one moment one look one touch one breath one cry
one prayer "i am jesús i have no last name so call
me jesús papote" his first words unnoticed by bells
midnight bells christmas day alley cat licking
wombs she slept she never felt maternal instinct
ultimate pain released for only she could give birth
for only she could experience red faced explosions
elevated to that sacrificial offering called life

vida life vida life vida death life death new birth
abraham sacrificed consciously she sacrificed sub-
consciously invisible ancestor of soledad he spoke:

My name is jesús papote i am born in oppression
my death a deeper martyrdom unknown to pain to
solitude to soledad to soledad's seven skins to
darkness to darkness' mystery to mystery's spirits.

My name is jesús papote i live nine months gut soul
i was addicted i was beaten i was kicked i was punched
i slept in empty cellars broken stairways i was infected i was injected spermed with many relations
i ran from police jails i was high every day of life
stabbing murders 1980 20th-century moon rockets micro-
magnetic computer operations 120-story edifices united
states instant replay future 21st-century advanced
new york the world lives in 1970 new york underdevel-
oped world in 1960 new york i am in 1980 new york
born around 18th-century abandoned structures
fighting to prevent broken scars from creating cancer
to my death.

My name is jesús papote born holy saturday easter
sunday march mother parading 3rd avenues' lower
streets car horns how much how long hotels
parking lots cellars men women elders new jersey
staten island connecticut long island all entered
my mother's secret veins 10 dollars 15 dollars i
was created ethnic sperm consortium's passionless
thrills social club more men entering more men entering i was conceived easter sunday resurrection
pagan abuses 1980 modern times.

She awoke she felt strange she relaxed the fix
had been applied nodding dance completed she
visited grandmother daisy flowers she could be
normal for a while folkloric mountain music
i met grandmother on my first day what an omen

grandma abuelita can you see me grandmother i
was the answer to your prayers your many unan-
swered prayers grandma i am alive can you see me
abuelita insisted to stay easter sunday veins
were pumping they take no vacation she had to
make the streets she walked past gossip's stares
abuelita felt ashamed abuelita felt herself nobody she had failed her daughter's baptism con-
firmation communion dignity pride virginity left
behind but she prayed even harder faith almighty
god not diminished candles the seven powers promises abuelita prayed her prayers made it easy
tonight . . . food rest spring walk she had to fight
the street she had refused the pimp's protection
she had to fight the corner she had no friends
she felt free tonight's crosscurrents open ethnic
music she felt something strange inside she walked
the glorious town central park rides broadway
nights bridges she looked across the waters ferry
evening lights statue of liberty's torch carrying
hand so strong wall street sunday silent newspaper
tonight tomorrow village open sexual society she
opinionated she knew new york's empty crevices
camera eyes recorded the instinct she felt strange
she felt something inside.

My name is jesús papote may month flowers she discovered me making her green throwing up she wanted
abortion she took pill after pill she had to wait
syphilis infection i came between the habit she
needed more i was an obstruction constant pressure
wrinkled inside cars in out constant pounding those
men were paying they had a right to hurt the habit
stronger tricks longer she became oral more and more
the money was not there one night nobody wanted her
she decided to extricate me she pounded punch after
punch like those men punch after punch abortion at
all costs she tired herself i lost my voice i supported her she was weak she could not move sitting

sidewalk cold cement she laid in bowery vagabonds
feeling her for nothing this was it she wanted no
more no more.

My name is jesús papote june cold turkey center cold
turkey her system must contain itself without chemi-
cals cold turkey naked unseasoned no taste unfeathered
cold turkey dry frozen human force battle begun fight
sweat shivers attacks in all directions cold turkey
intravenous coup d'etat demanding charging torturing
nuclear blasts invasions delirium opiate roots electric
shocks kidnapping she threw up the world she greened
she scratched-drew-blood nails on scars scabbing
pores blood vessels eruptions hands on blood she
painted open mental torture digging into wall's
electricity cabled concussion paralyzing currents
she wrote god let me die god let me die she fought
we fought i was not an added burden i kept quiet
i held if she survived detoxified normal life no
more deserted streets no more pains no more misery
she won grandma she won she smiled she ate she
beat the odds.

My name is jesús papote 4th of july celebration
plane ride across to puerto rico mountain house
utuado high up clear nights future dreams new
life breathings caribbean enchanted nation long
rides past guajataca splendored beaches arecibo's
indian caves dorado evenings she entered san juan
white cemetery patriots resting singing to la
perla pearled down old spanish architecture el
morro distanced open sea curving palm trees tick-
ling skies connecting sea-breezing moon san juan
song folklore painting after painting came alive
leo-mildness-august night tidal waves moving bells
quietly sunset lowering her thighs cooled refreshed
stimulated sauna touches moon-lit beauty mark smiled
sun met in ocean eclipse mistress round-up night
after night shimmering fresh air slow pace coastal

sand walk fresh fruit pineapple spicy fish coconut
nights kissing early morning mango blossoms new sun
octapusing rays orange rainbows the ox-cart was your
solution your final triumph how beautiful you look
inside the western sunset phosphorous bay shining
artesian ponce musically carved saints flamboyant
trees luquillo beach preparations into rain forest
deities once lived they greet us they talk loíza
carnaval blackness río grande julia de burgos phrasings oh mamita i was so afraid oh mamita stay in
taíno mountains caguana-shaped symbol of cemí oh
mamita don't go back give birth in island nativeness
tropical greetings nurturing don't go back don't
go back.

My name is jesús papote september pregnant body new
york spells trouble once-again-racing-fast struggles
rapid fire pellets struggles pouring anxieties 18th-
century remnants immigrant struggles spanish second-
third-class citizens struggles education non-existent
struggles companion song of destiny struggles spell
troubles.

My name is jesús papote she october tried training
program cellar jobs she vowed not to use it again
columbus was discovered he discovered gold discovered competition discovered defeat discovered lack
of opportunity halloween witch creeping in she said
no she said no strong they came back she said no
strong ugly cursed evil she said no strong she felt
pains i was restless i was acting up i had relapsed
i was choking i needed it she said no she said no
strong i was in pain she said no yes no yes no no
urgings yes yes achings no no yes no yes no yes
stubbornly she said no she said no she said no
strong.

My name is jesús papote november all souls day
grandma knocked on door oh no the prayers fell

defeated once again pain killers sleeping face
hallway scrambling avenues putrid dope stumbles
nightsticks digging digging deep spinal corded
night 300 dollars pure divinity bombarded atomic
explosions final war coma death radiation pellets
death la muerte sneaking in no breath feelings
death la muerte coming after us moving fast
death la muerte assured us she was winning
death la muerte doctors priests last testament
death la muerte trying to save me over my mother
death la muerte she refused her strength engulfed
death la muerte doorbell of fear
death la muerte abusing us unfairly
death la muerte nothing could be done
death la muerte divine hope of all living things
death was spitting its steel claws earthquake
we attacked her we fought her we prevented her
from penetrating our testicles we pulled her
intestines her naked slimy body we switch bladed
cuts across her face we rumbled into her adam's
apple biting into her senses we squeezed her
obnoxious overweight loose teeth cancer we cut her
breasts we raped her we mugged her we escaped her we
iced her thanksgiving fiesta carved with delight
we were eating seasoned turkey triumph champagne
toast to that ultimate desire to live live vivir.

My name is jesús papote december christmas
new york city my inner cycle 9 months completed what
a life what a life my mother's mouth once again
on elder's variety theatre 2 dollars 40 mouths
every day christmas eve day oh sweet sour destiny
ghetto sacrifice wounded limbs tears surfacing
loneliness soledad seven skins solitude underneath
sub-vulgate open concubines society condones it
society has not cured itself from it society cannot
outlaw such misery right there for future children
to see to watch to fear right there in front of
little angels in naked open spaces oh but sad lonely

night dear savior's birth long lay the world in
sin 'til he appeared thrill of hope save him jesus
alley cats symphony save him jesus abandoned tenement
screaming save him jesus indians buried inside cement
chanting save him jesus she did not hear final cry:

Mami Mami push push i'm coming out celestial barkings
Mami Mami push i don't want to die she slept
Mami Mami push i want to live she slept cough
Mami Mami i have the ability to love cough cough
Mami Mami fight with me again she slept she slept
Mami Mami i'm coming out out out push push push push
Mami Mami can you feel me can you hear me push push
push push empuja empuja cough cough push push push
empuja empuja Mami cough cough push push i am fighting
i am fighting push push nature nature i have a will
to live to denounce you nature i am fighting by myself
your sweeping breasts your widowing backbone
yearnings your howling cemetery steps your
death-cold inhuman palms Mami Mami wake up
this is my birthday little mornings king
david sang cough cough cough push push
why do I have to eulogize myself
nobody is listening i am invisible
why tell me why do i have to be
the one the one to acclaim that:

   We, nosotros, compassionate caring people
   We, nosotros, respectful of spanish-english forms
   We, nosotros, peace in mind tranquility
   We, nosotros, inside triangle of contradictions
   We, nosotros, nation-feeling-total-pride
   We, nosotros, strong men powerful women loving children
   We, nosotros, hispanic hemispheric majority
   We, nosotros, latinos million bicultural humanists
   We, nosotros, folkloric mountain traditionalists
   We, nosotros, spanish tongue culture older than english
   We, nosotros, conceiving english newer visions
   We, nosotros, multi-ethnic black-brown-red in affirmations

We, nosotros, ghetto brothers black americans indians
              italians irish jewish polish ukrainians
              russian german food and music lovers
We, nosotros, mathematicians of the magical undocumented
              dollar architects of close-knit spaces
We, nosotros, 5th largest foreign market we consumed
              all the goods 83 years association of
              goods we fought world wars decorated up
              front to meet the fresh-troop enemy
We, nosotros, oral poets transcending 2 european forms
              spanish dominance when spanish was strong
              english dominance when english was strong
              we digested both we absorbed the pregnancies
              we stand at crossroads 21st-century new man
              great-grandfathers chornos-spirits sing
              with me allow me this one last wish limbo
              baptism of faith this one last christmas
              moment to my mother who doesn't answer

with the permission of all the faiths of all beliefs
with the permission of this land
with the permission of the elders
with the permission of english
with the permission of my community
with the permission of god:

      allow this spanish word to be understood
      i ask for your silence for language is
      always understood in any sentiment
      with your permission Mami
      i ask for one gift one magi gift
      inside these heavy odds
      there is a spanish word
      spanish ultimate of words
      that will survive
      there is a puerto rican
      blessing universal to the world
      hear it is only for you
      for i love you i don't blame you

i am also responsible for state
of being, so with this, my only
breath, my last wind, my last
supper sentiment, i tell you
with pride that i am proud to
have been your son, to have come
from you, with the tenderness
of my grandmother's prayers,
with the silent love of all my
people, with the final resolution
of our nationhood, i am asking
for my blessings BENDICIÓN
BEN . . . DI . . . CI . . . ÓN

she woke up she saw she startled she warmed she
protected she cried she broke the umbilical cord
she got up to follow the bells the bells the bells
cats dogs vagabonds all followed the tinkle tinkle
of the bells christmas bells nativity flowing bells
faith hope and charity bells 1980 jesus christ and
jesús papote midnight ecstasy of bells church steps
door opens organ stops up the aisle she exclaimed
jesús papote human legacy god the son at the right
hand holy spirit candles flowers incense wine water
and finally the people grandmother she offered jesús
papote to the people miracle cherubim flautists
dancing and singing rejoice rejoice eternity smiles
oh night divine oh night divine she knelt she smiled
jesús papote's presence in the dignity of our lives.

little man

awfully quiet this saturday morning
americanita placing book on shelves
she observed up-tight librarian
divinity-walking air sternly
out the central door.

awfully quiet this saturday morning
americanita alone except for little man
it was so secretive so quiet
so out of touch with neighborhood
so old so pretty so well preserved
so mysterious so beautifully lonely
so silent that . . .
they kissed
and tongue kissed
and played with fingers
so quietly romantic
underneath the literature section
carrying-on worthy of
instant chapters
library tabernacles
pleasing with delight . . .

serious dude

Yes, sí, i like her, y qué,
what's wrong with that?
I don't care who she's in love with,
i'm in love with her,
i'm not going to deny it, bro,
yo no lo voy a negar, so what, so,
i'll never kiss her, that's okay too,
but i dig the way she walks,
i mean she walks like finger-snapping
church bells on summer conga drums
playing clave on time, yes, sí
i want her, y qué, it's not her,
it's me, it's my fantasies, bro,
it's what turns me on, it's about
my dreams, and so what if she never
kisses me, hey, you can't have everything, but i know one thing, she'll
live with my memory, i'm not afraid
to tell her that i love her, i want
her to feel strong and secure, i
want her to feel strong and secure,
that somebody likes her, you dig,
whoever likes her will know that
i like her too, and when she looks
at herself, she'll know i'm there,
bro, and, in her private moments,
i know i make her happy, you dig,
i know because i'm bad, that's why,
because i treat her with respect,
that's why, and i live with la
esperanza, hey, that one day, un día,
she will walk my proud jitterbug
down this vecindario, brother-man,
i'm waiting, bro, i'm waiting, bro,
this is soul gut, my man, so
remember, if she wants me, i expect
you to step aside, bro, i mean that,
serious.

tito madera smith

(for dr. juan flores)

he claims he can translate palés matos'
black poetry faster than i can talk,
and that if i get too smart,
he will double translate pig latin
english right out of webster's
dictionary, do you know him?

he claims he can walk into east harlem
apartment where langston hughes gives
spanglish classes for newly arrived
immigrants seeking a bolitero-numbers
career and part-time vendors of cuchi-
fritters sunday afternoon in central
park, do you know him?

he claims to have a stronghold of the
only santería secret baptist sect in
west harlem, do you know him?

he claims he can talk spanish styled in
sunday dress eating crabmeat-jueyes
brought over on the morning eastern
plane deep fried by la negra costoso
joyfully singing puerto rican folklore: plena NR
"maría luisa no seas brava,
llévame contigo pa la cama," or
"oiga capitán delgado, hey captain delgaro,
mande a revisar la grama, please inspect
the grass, que dicen que un aeroplano,
they say that an airplane throws marijuana
seeds."

do you know him? yes you do,
i know you know him, that's right,
madera smith, tito madera smith:
he blacks and prieto talks at the same time,

splitting his mother's santurce talk,
twisting his father's south carolina soul,
adding new york scented blackest harlem
brown-eyes diddy bops, tú sabes mami,
that i can ski like a bomba soul salsa
mambo turns to aretha franklin stevie
wonder nicknamed patato guaguancó steps,
do you know him?

he puerto rican talks to las mamitas
outside the pentecostal church, and
he gets away with it, fast-paced i
understand-you-my-man, with clave
sticks coming out of his pockets hooked
to his stereophonic 15-speaker indispensable
disco sounds blasting away at cold reality
struggling to say estás buena baby
as he walks out of tune and out of
step with alleluia cascabells,
puma sneakers,
pants rolled up,
shirt cut in middle chest,
santería chains,
madamo pantallas, *pendients*
into the spanish social club,
to challenge elders in dominoes,
like the king of el diario's
budweiser tournament
drinking cerveza-beer
like a champ,
do you know him?
well, i sure don't,
and if i did, i'd
refer him to 1960
social scientists
for assimilation
acculturation
digging
autopsy

into
their
heart
attacks,
oh,
oh,
there
he
comes,
you can call him tito,
or you can call him madera,
or you can call him smitty,
or you can call him mr. t.,
or you can call him nuyorican,
or you can call him black,
or you can call him latino,
or you can call him mr. smith,
his sharp eyes of awareness,
greeting us in aristocratic harmony:
"you can call me many things, but
you gotta call me something."

juana (bochisme) *invención chisme.*

ay virgen, mira que si fulana de tal estaba anoche
con juan de los parlotes, metida en un carro y,
tú sabes, la dejaron a tres cuadras de la esquina,
dicen que era el boss de la factoría,
y lo más peor, salió con las, tú sabes, toda estrujá. . . .
santa maría purísima, y que pegándole cuernos al pobre juan pueblo
simplemente porque lo vio salir de una barra a las tres de la mañana,
esa escusa como que no suena bien ¿verdad?
en serio, no te miento, carlos cocina le metió tremenda pescosá
en pleno baile porque bailó merengue con un dominicano,
eso le pasa por ser presentá. . . .
y la victoria ascensor, me dijo manny parque
que lo oyó de tito esquina que lo habían llamado de puerto rico,
te lo juro, lo que pasa en nueva york inmediatamente lo saben en
      manatí,
se me perdió el hilo . . . sí, ajá, es así,
¿te das cuenta del revolú con pedro edificio?
la rosa cuarto sin vergüenza lo choteó con el housing
de su jugada de gallo en el quinto piso de los proyectos,
pero existe un detalle que no está claro,
según las lenguas por ahí,
me dijeron del bochinche con estrella avenida,
esa mujer rompecasa fuerza de cara corteja de pablo escalera,
¿puedes tú creer semejante cosa?
ella le quita los cheques del social security
mientras vive con pedro rufo en un hotel de brooklyn,
y le saca otro cheque a la welfare con una dirección de staten
      island . . .
y ¿qué me dices de la petra sala?, tiene una tienda de food stamps,
se ha hecho millonaria vendiendo bolita en tres condados,
guiada de viuda, soltera y divorciá,
comprando casa en puerto rico sin pagar presupuestos,
y si tú la vieras, la llorona teresa azotea,
pues, ahora te cuento, fíjate,
le quitó los chavos al enclenco flaco aquel que estaba en la fiesta,
¿te recuerdas?, sí, ése mismo, óyeme,
y después lo amenazó con el bartender mañoso del social club,

hijo de uno de sus queridos, amigo de su ex-amante,
con tanto revolú y traqueteo, no sabes tú el dolor de cabeza
que a mí me da para memorizarme el garabato pan de gato
que existe en el tercer piso de mi edificio,
te digo que el welfare me debe pagar overtime. . . .
pero no te he contado el último descaro,
mario se viste de maría cuando viene el social worker,
y jesús acera me dijo que la pepa bolita
hizo un brujo con una haitiana,
¿sabes para quién?, imagínate tú, pues, para mí,
ella dijo que yo era una lengüilarga, si yo fuera lengüilarga
te diría que ella es una marimacha apestosa, pero yo,
inmediatamente me fui a la espiritista y me limpié,
por eso vine aquí primero a contarte todo esto,
ya que no te gusta hablar pero que te encanta oír,
bueno, me voy, ay virgen, si ya es tiempo de cocinar,
tengo que avanzar, me esperan en el 360, el 430 y pico,
la bodega, la lavandería, tendré que hablar entre novelas,
cómo se va el tiempo, dios santo.

unemployment line

pablo pueblo city man, unemployed man, stands 20th in line,
pablo pueblo city man, unemployed man, stands 15th in line,
pablo pueblo city man, unemployed man, stands 5th in line,
pablo pueblo city man, unemployed man, stands first in line,
on the unemployment circle:

¿usted me puede atender? *(cantando)*
¿usted me puede atender?
he esperado en esta línea,
y aunque yo no sepa inglés,
deme deme el privilegio,
de acercarme hacia usted,
oiga usted, me puede atender,
un trabajo yo quiero obtener,

yo vengo de la cantera,
por el paso de un avión,
aquí en el sur bronx llegué,
a buscar una fortuna,
y aprender un poco inglés,
oiga usted, ¿me puede atender?

me mandaron aquí ayer,
me mandaron allá antier,
y antes de ayer, el mes se fue,
pasaron tres, ya tengo diez,
me encuentro abajo y deprimido,
oiga usted, ¿me puede atender?

¿usted me puede atender?
¿usted me puede atender?
¿usted me puede atender?

después de esta letanía,
hablé con la señorita de este bembé,
y ella con una risa que no era linda,
con una gracia que era maldita,

me dijo así, así, así:
"please speak in english
speak english sir,
don't understand a word you say,
speak english sir,
don't understand a word you say."

¿usted me puede atender?, me caso en diez,
¿usted me puede atender?, me caso en diez,
basta ya, atiéndame,
basta ya, atiéndame,
atiéndame, atiéndame,
basta ya.

pablo pueblo city man, unemployed man, stands outside
the unemployment circle, they made a check for him
on the spot.

bolita folktale

one-thirty south bronx tale took form,
don julio silently dreamed, "pegarse"
feelings digested in "pensamientos,"
paradise bar otb/numbers don q conversations,
pedro jukebox navaja blading latino tragedy.

two-thirty el barrio tale took form,
el mudo rushed into paradise bar,
nine fingers in the air, "el nueve,"
don julio's good luck dream,
927 san juan street,
don julio woke to play 927 today.

three-thirty brooklyn tale took form,
el mudo rushed into paradise bar,
two fingers in the air, "el dos,"
tensión in don julio's smile,
bolita payoffs on number 2 at 8 to 1,
brooklyn, manhattan, múcura at night,
don julio had the 927 going,
bruni the barmaid excited,
the smell of 1000 "pescados" at stake,
rounds of "salud, buena suerte, agua
florida, santa bárbara" crossing
fingers for number 7 to come out.

four-thirty loisaida tale took form,
el mudo rushed into paradise bar,
seven fingers in the air, "el siete,"
don julio's back gleefully showered
with "aprietos" peeling open bar,
free drinks, kissing cheeks, many
payoffs on lucky 7 at 8 to 1,
el mudo jumping and dancing,
he took the number, hotel will be paid.

five-thirty new york spinal corded,
celebration turned sour, Pedro el
Bolitero carne in, not feeling ecstatic,
quickly reminding don julio, the 927
was for manhattan, he played brooklyn,
drowning jubilation turned apologetic
broken pockets lifetiming "ava maría,
qué mala suerte, por poco, por un hilo,
no te apures, juega
combinao la próxima vez, la suerte te
vendrá, ten fe, ya tú verás."

six o'clock south bronx tale took form,
don julio playing 927 for manhattan múcura,
thinking of a smarter bet, another dream,
the better odds, inside the sunset of a
new york city night.

abandoned building

LA VIDA es un español derretido
        un frío escalofrío
        donde el sol solamente
        acaricia mi rota realidad
        reñida entre la
        urbe americana y
        un barrio corazón
        latino.

LA VIDA es un folklore de pueblo
        jíbaro encarretado en
        televisiones dominadas
        del sabor ron coca-cola
        bolita bachata juego y
        sudor.

LA VIDA es una derrota en la escuela
        un sobretrabajo mal pagado
        un amor tierno y fuerte
        donde las necesidades se
        vacían en el cuerpo de
        la esperanza.

LA VIDA es un inglés frío
        un español no preciso
        un spanglish disparatero
        una inseguridá de
        incendios automáticos.

LA VIDA es pues, mi pana, LA VIDA es
        un dolor de muela
        mellada en el hueco
        seno cáncer, sin remedio,
        parada en el cemento,
        de esta triste,
        mi desnuda realidad.

olga pecho

yo me batallo
con la vida
apuesto 200 pesos
cuando viene el cheque
yo me vuelvo loca
jugando barajas
hasta que me esnúen
black jack por chupones
si sale 21 a mano negra
tengo que meterle mano
a la jodedera en las
azoteas del basement
con el corazón empinao
a lo cool-cool marimacha
del destino.
si gano gano si pierdo
pues pierdo pero hay
que tirarse a pecho hay
que jugarse la vida el
primero del mes de todos
los días yo me las juego
con cualquiera.
ya la gente me respeta
saben que no hay más na.

maría ciudad

era la luz de la mañana,
triste y sola se encontraba,
otro día, mil apuros,
otro día, sin descanso.

en su reflejo ella buscaba,
fuerza, aliento, en su espada,
para batallar la vida entera
hasta papel de hombre ella jugaba.

a las potencias les rogó,
se llenó de inspiración,
a sus hijos levantó,
a la escuela, a su futuro.

maquinillando se encontró,
trabajó con mucho orgullo,
era la fuente de energía,
y sus compañeros, así se lo decían:

maría en las ciudades, fuerte se veía
confrontaba las situaciones,
llena en progreso, llena de vida.

almorzaba en el teléfono,
cuentas a plazo, cuido en niños,
a las cinco ella corría
a preparar la cena,
y adorar a sus hijos,
y el sol, el sol, el sol medio dormido,
maría ciudad, a ella admiró,
con su rojo colorido,
por las calles le cantó:

maría en las ciudades, fuerte se veía,
confrontaba las situaciones,
llena en progreso, llena de vida.

era dura, era fuerte,
era brava y protectiva,
el amor si viene viene,
después que mis deberes
estén cumplidos,
en la noche descanso,
se miró en su reflejo,
y aquí lo íntimo llegó,
y a su amante ella llamó.

maría en las ciudades, fuerte se veía,
confrontaba las situaciones,
llena en progreso, llena de vida:

¡maría ciudad!
¡maría ciudad!
¡maría ciudad!

puerto rican

silk
smooth
ivory
polished
into
brown
tan
black
soul
leaning
back
looking
proud
sharp
answers
casual
community
conversations
based
in
mental
admiration
how
highly
we
claim
our
worth
conceiving
new
society
inside
cemented
hard
core

beauty
chanting
snapping
beats

familia

moments personal worth,
life ceases for a minute,
pays attention to a milestone.

moments when choke of tear,
adam's apple above the eye.

moments when sacrifices find glory.

moments when we come together,
everlasting kinship strength.

moments when ay bendito humanity
flourishes and expands.

and of course,

moments when family tree
sees nuclear-expanded
attention moving upward,
abuelita at the center
of the trust.

sky people
(*la gente del cielo*)

eye-scratching mountain view
Puerto Rico counting houses
upon houses, hill after hill,
in valleys and in peaks,
to observe: la gente del cielo,
fingering on clouds,
climbing further and further,
to preserve taíno folklore,
gente del cielo,
toiling the land,
art crafting musical symbols,
giving birth to more angelitos del cielo,
whose open-spaced hands captured moon waltz:
solemn serenity serenading life,
la gente del cielo,
who prayed in nature's candlelight,
galaxies responding with milky way guiñaítas
winked in tropical earth smile,
as God gleefully conceded,
what we had perceived all along,
that Puerto Rico is 100 by 35 by 1000
mountains multiplied by the square root
of many cultures breathing: ONE.

diega

diega llega, diega arrives, diega legacies,
diega llega, diega portrays, diega street-smarts,

diega llega, diega understands, diega loves. . . .

what more can i say about your soft strokes
caricias screaming gently on a smile.

what more can i say about your gracious
saludos hometown sentimientos mountain
jibarita romantic melody of songs streaming
from your lips memories yearning from your
soul.

what more can i say, diega, how easy to say
your name, tu nombre, no pretensions,
no ornaments, saying simply diega, easy to
reach, easy to touch, dulce-soft silk
embroidered symphony your voice chanting
dancing living a cali, your cali, diega.

diega, you have arrived a otra etapa,
another time, but need not worry mamita,
you can sing to us the winds at night
are waiting, and we will speak your
caring phrases protecting our hands,
inspiring our eyes, stimulating our
senses.

diega, woman, mother, simplicity in
every sound you syllabled to us,
what more, diega, what more than
essence kissing petals on our
foreheads, never to be forgotten
affection, the rivers, the mountains,
the heavens, you touched us, you hugged

us, deeply, freely, diega, diega,
we respect your presence,
your children grandchildren
tataranietos and chornos of the future . . .

te recordamos en el presente, bendición,
vieja, you diega, opening the door of
st. peter, festive celebration in the
gates of your eternity and this Barrio
that you touched.

Oro in Gold

flutist

she
sprayed
golden
syllables
angelic
whistle
calls
gently
phrasing
musical
notes
fingering
celestial
innocence
inside
warm
lonely
nights
waiting
for
the
serenade

sand

finely grained
crystals sea-polished
weightless granules
salt water aging rocks
planted smoothly
naked grounds
inviting evening's
open bosoms
flawless winds
riding breezes
tidal waves
mistress
lover-nights
shaped mountain
craters moon-love
yearnings
pregnant
nature's
many periods
virgin fragility
as in french
talk making
love.

just before the kiss

canela brown sugar coated bomboncitos
melting deliciously upon a sweet tooth tongue;
canela brown gold dust on top of tembleque;
canela brown fine sticks to flavored cocoa;
canela grounded into arroz con dulce;
canela melao
canela dulce.

canela browned in deep tan caribbean
sweet lips almost sabroso tasted by
a cariñoso sentiment, y buena que estás,
en gusto affection that cries
out loud: qué chévere tú eres,
como canela brown warrior woman diplomática
with her terms.

all of this canela,
inside your luscious lips,
smooth phrasing me deeeeply,
waking me up on the middle-night,
to change from exclamation mark
into an accent accenting:
canela, mi negra,
canela, trigueña,
canela, mulata,
canela, mi prieta,
bésame,
to taste your
cinnamon
powdered
tongue.

standards

in order for you to touch me,
you would have to convince me,
you respect my all, my ambitions,
my beliefs, for you to touch me,
you must allow freedom to my space,
you must express human sincerity,
detest gluttony and greed,
but if i say touch me,
you have won my heart,
i will take your universe beyond,
i will talk incessantly into your ears,
i will caress your limb's existence,
so suave, touch,
so smooth, touch, touch,
sweet
smells
sensored
sensual
sensations
saturated
softly
smoothly
seducing
sensitive
stems
slowly

scenting
sensuous
touch, oh, touch, deep in
    divino, divina,
    qué bueno
       libertad

velluda: alliterated y eslembao

it was all about my fingers, each one of them:
    el meñique se figuraba fuerte
    fabulosamente fermentando figuras
    fraternales en el rocío de tu boca.
it was all about my fingers, each one of them:
    el anular circulando cuadros
    concéntricos cariñosamente
    caminando por el pecho en tus
    montañas.
it was all about my fingers, each one of them:
    el del corazón suavizando sen-
    sualmente sobos sexuales suspirando
    en las venas de tu vientre.
it was all about my fingers, each one of them:
    el índice lubricando lazos lucientes
    en las ramas de tus piernas,
and finally, mi negra,
it was all about my fingers, each one of them:
    el pulgar hincándose íntimamente
    ilustrándose en las bases
    de tus raíces.
i came down, all the way down,
completing nurture
then you, mulata, you gave
birth to my hands, which
you caressed until the
touches tinkled stars of
delight as you introduced
me to your universe:
    velluda: alliterated y eslembao,
    i got lost inside your rain forest.

the patria in my borinquen

that i stumbled into my spring walk
wrinkled seven years many night brawls
marijuanated lover calls forcing you
to give it up give it all up your
poetry drowsing passionless pleasures
scar-faced avenue walk.

all of a sudden i met my puppy love
across the street washed up skinny
body i searched searched transformed:

> teenage summer central park
> in my eyes you aristocratic virgin
> in your eyes me creative wind
> we exchange love poems
> i gave in you gave in you
> undid me i trembled the numbered
> poems delicate poetic spanglish
> grammatically sensing me
> you bit i bit we bit the grass
> your lips gave me puertoricanness
> intimately transformed transformed:

i face your loisaida air struggling to move
bones crushing facing adversity hard times
suffering times, and for a macho moment i
thought i was your beauty your positive
strength i went after you running screaming
liberating your chains, "patria, you are my
borinquen; patria, you are my borinquen,"
you turned around, my spirit felt relaxed,
you were strong enough to overcome all
obstacles, mi patria, and still leave
borinquen taína poetry to
caress heart world

penetration
(*to sandra esteves/julia de burgos*)

the day julia de burgos came back
to project herself into modern existence
to announce sister-love for poet-woman
whose tranquility was amputated by a
ricocheted bullet infiltrating spiritual
vibration bullet exploding in direction
of taína woman two children abreast
inside sad desperation abandoned building
caves only to miss the bus only to feel
mother-father struggles street-walking
alone.

> the day julia de burgos came back out
> of alcoholic liver busting along street
> corner resurrection was to intersect
> interject face hand heart rejecting
> pellets penetrating sandra's children
> skulls.

but sandra felt cone-shaped steel
penetrating soft-shelled skin
preventing her from carrying
children now astounded grimacing
pain mami's llantos lowering
face hand heart neck knees
surrendering petals demon's bite
blessing cold-deep sidewalk's
sorrowful turmoil.

> julia de burgos watched in pain
> remembering her day she inspired
> sandra to combat to denounce to
> demand thorough examination, no

more wasteful deaths, no more
bullets from destitute society,
deaths will be natural, deaths
will be patriotic confrontation.

then, julia de burgos went to
puerto rico, to lolita lebrón
novena-praying for many sandra
marías avenging in every meditation in every act of life
the grips of those whose pellets
wanted to control puerto rican
women's self-destiny.

compañera
(*for susana*)

entre el conjunto, compañera,
el patriotismo-siempre-vive
en la historia puertorriqueña.

entre el sonido, compañera,
noches largas después del
trabajo atravesando barrios
llevando claridades puertorriqueñas.

entre comillas, compañera,
hablar claro poderoso
respeto de razas y cultura
nueva realidad puertorriqueña.

entre mis frases, compañera,
sociedades libres de dueños
envidiosos.

entre la verdá, sí, más que sí, compañera,
adentro de un festejo, dos vasos de vino,
dos fuertes abrazos, una comunidad
puertorriqueña.

y al fin,

>   entre las gotas de sudor,
>   entre el don de un amor fiel,
>   entre el cariño libre de mentiras,
>   entre el beso firme y sensual
>   entre nuestros hermanos, compañera.

Prendas

alicia alonso

absolutamente
ascendiendo
acrobáticamente
al
aire
acariciando
abiertamente
al
amor
al
ayer
al
ángel
arropado
antes
al
andar
habanero
amaneciendo
abajo
atendiendo
al
amor

suni paz

el son y la paz
debajo se ven un
cello celando el
le lo lai como
si picasso hubiera
nacido en borinquen
tierra un cello cielo
jibarito llamando la
flauta que toque cayey
cibao andes panamá
venezuela méjico en
una sola nota de son
y paz debajo se ve un
cello cielo celando
como que el otoño no
existe porque suni
canta argentina por
los barrios de esperanza
que hasta la conga se
desviste desde el cielo
y descansa su dolor

vaya, carnal

sabes, pinche, que me visto
estilo zoot suit marca de
pachuco royal chicano air
force montoyado en rojo
azul verde marrón nuevo
callejero chicano carnales
eseándome como si el ése ése
echón que se lanza en las
avenidas del inglés con
treinta millones de batos
locos hablando en secreto
con el chale-ése-no-la-chingues
vacilón a los gringos americanos,
¿sabes?, simón, el sonido del este,
el vaya, clave, por la maceta,
que forma parte de un fuerte
lingüismo, raza, pana, borinquen,
azteca, macho, hombre, pulmones
de taíno, de indios, somos
chicano-riqueños, qué curada,
simón, que quemada mi pana,
la esperanza de un futuro
totalmente nuestro,
tú sabes, tú hueles,
el sabor, el fervor del
vaya, carnal.

john forever

"ten minutes of silence." . . . yoko

poetry haiku lyrics
filled with universal stanzas
music mirrors depth in visions
bonded chains harmony;
morning lines rhythmic phrases
singing night stars beads of sorrows
sensing smiling spirit feelings
loving songs hearts at ease:

> john of peace, john of peace
> john of peace, john of peace
> john of peace, john of peace
> sing, sing, sing
> john of peace, john of peace
> john of peace, john of peace
> john of peace, john of peace
> john of peace, john of peace
> john of peace:
>
> john forever, we espouse you
> john forever, we espouse you
> john forever, we espouse you
> sing your songs
> deep john sing:

sunday vigil not to worship
but to light a burning candle
tender loving skies of people
praying peace world at ease
closing eyes in meditation
yearning love winds deep sensations
chanting, humming, singing, whispering,
many tongues in one breeze:

john of peace, john of peace . . .
john forever, we espouse you
john forever, we espouse you
john forever, we espouse you
sing your songs
deep john sing. . . .

miriam makeba

place choice seat struggle sings africa:
celestial adjectives trumpets announce her entrance
verbs god's actions conjunction mountains
nouns rained phrases people's interjections
unified inside adverbs her tongue.

prepositions souled third world exclamation
applauses pronouns inside voice vernacular
ten languages one tone nativeness royal
presence odaro-greetings first born oral
expressions genuflecting richness.

she soul flows way back beginning of color
blackness veined seven continents everything complacent they brought original back
new faces disturbing devils prostitution
presenting different version original life
civilization beginning-noise alphabets were
noises before adam's apple colonizers
sacrificed seven natural elements water sun
fire storm day night moon death praised oya
ogoun ochoun obatalá elleggua changó yemayá
reactions closest to god nature cannot be
controlled she shakes foundations tears
underneath drums constantly beating sending
messages whooping voice angers soothes
satisfies voice wastes no words meaningless-
ness cleansed tones eyes hearts tongues
fingers emotions breathtaking swelling veins.

her mood softens transforms mountain scene
africa seething beauty shadows earth skies
sun arrive heaven grounds queen soul queen
gentleness queen freedom festal universal
nigeria looking soul people dreaming stars
god's warriors liberating black lands
transformation taking place majority rule

home rule africa of age spirits speak strong
leaders seven powers raging black red cannot
stumble nigeria proud concert singer roots
in ritual universally understood culture.

her ultimate song release promise movements
promise rootness promise physical sacrifice
death for love promise looking each other
profound togetherness making it in all ways
of love in all ways of love in all ways and
manners of capable love in all ways and
expressions physical to love in all physical
spiritual mannerisms describing love alone
under sole star africa.

rafa

as triangular ship deposited blacks
caribbean molasses deposited blacks
for slavery and cotton;

as black african preserved original
culture inside christianity he was
forced to swallow;

as the puerto rican challenged
drums to bomba step's endurance
strength drummers against dancers;

as they created plena rhythms
to news events on southern ponce
streets;

as they searched for recognition
since 1500 finally melting into
puerto rican folklore;

as it all came down to rafael
cortijo playing bomba and plena
many piñones of my childhood;

as he finally exploded 1960
ismael rivera sounds puerto
rican charts creating music
the world over;

as we search through plena history
there's a godfather-padrino-figure
humble but stubborn to his traditions;

as we detail contributions
so must we all stand
gracious ovation
rafael cortijo
unanimous consensus
puerto rican people.

juan boria

hay que comenzar, de negro prieto mulato,
caciques que se derriten bomba-plena tumbando;
sí, hay que comenzar, en voz celeste africana,
sol negrura borinqueña, compás de pueblo cantando;
sí, hay que comenzar, en noche misterio maraña,
cocolos tambores rezando, ritos trigueños asaltando;
sí, hay que comenzar, a piel de esquinillero,
al vaya folklore hermano, miren lo que trajo el barco,
un puertorro declamando, nació un negro, nació un negro,
nació estirao, vestido de blanco, sabe usted,
nació y que pitando él alabado del nalgueo,
la comadrona grita, "un milagro,"
señores nació recitando rumbeando,
miren se paró de paso a paso,
pique en punta, bailando mambo,
oigan, señores, la virgen bendice, "un milagro,"
el barrio entero gritando, santurce, ponce,
hasta el gallo cucuruqueando, vengan, está aquí,
el director ejecutivo de la bemba burocracia,
huracán en remolino, un nuevo diccionario,
casabes, jueyes, cerezas, cogen panderetas en manos,
al on de la o, en la e de la i, la u son-pulso del compás
a empezar, a terminar   juan juan
palesmatear y guillenear   juan juan
con su gracia, su sonrisa   juan juan
su alta voz de melodía   juan juan
que comience el festejo,
lechón, morcilla, alcapurrias,
guineítos, salmorejo, ron llave,
coquito, lechosa, pasteles,
bacalaítos, la yuca y el ñame,
que venga la serenata, noche santa,
el presidente-comandante-caballero,
recitando al todo negro,
de la cuna con sus versos.

homenaje a don luis palés matos

retumba el pasado presente prosa poesía
retumba el calor sudor vaivenes de cuero
salpicando mares olor tambor prieto quemao
orgullos cadereando acentos al español
conspiración engrasando ritmos pleneros
a la lengua española pa ponerle sabor.

pero que retumba en la tumba resbalando
pico pico tun tun de pasa áfrica se pierde
en puerto rico tirando pasos nichos a los santos
marcando al uno dos en tres por cuatro
que alientan los versos exaltan los salmos
despierta la clave chupando las cañas
pracutú-piriquín-prucú-tembandeando
el secreto máximo: que luis palés matos
también era grifo africano guillao de castellano.

qué de blanco:

> era un grifo babalao oba-rey guayamesano,
> salió de *sspirita* mulata liberada,
> fue un trabajo de pueblo una noche secreta,
> cogieron un ñáñigo *espíritu* lui,
> que espiraba a ser blanco,
> con un tumbao celestial lenguas dos razas,
> lo bautizaron palés añadieron el matos,
> dios la pava omnipresente sacude exprime:
> el trabajo, antillano, carifricano,
> afro-españolisao, manteca sal y vinagre, y
> de pronto se despierta un alma, un alma,
> que alientan los cuerpos, maniobrando,
> cabecita pa arriba, manitas pa' lado,
> deditos en clave, pechito pa fuera, y salió:
>
> un negrindio sureño, rascacielo de mulato,
> patología criolla, ogoun-ochoun de barrio,
> otun-derecha de la danza,

[handwritten annotations: "> grifen? (libro de Palés)."; "→ ritmos de clave"; "(palabra inventada x Palés)"; "jazz poetry en inglés"]

caracol cangrejo yemayado,
conocedor imprudente africano,
usted y tenga poeta antillano,
betún del brillo borincano,
pracutú-priniquín-prucú-tembandeando
el secreto máximo: que luis palés matos
también era grifo africano guillao de castellano.

cultura afrocaribeñ?.

bomba, para siempre

(cauiión)

↳ base de la salsa

bomba: we know we are electricity, we know we are a sun:
bomba: bring in the jazz, and merengue, blend africa:
bomba: puerto rican history for always, national pride:
bomba: cadera beats, afternoon heat, sunday beach:
bomba: we all came in, negritos bien lindos:
bomba: center space, intact beauty, rhythmic pride:
bomba: compose the cheo song lucecita sings curet smiles:
bomba: and once again bomba: se queda allí bomba:

(coro comunidad)

    un negrito melodía he came along,
    improvising bomba drums on dancer's feet,
    choral songs, sonero heat, snapping hands,
    sweat at ease, melodía sang,
    he sang like this:

→   se queda allí, se queda allí, se queda allí, es mi raíz.

    los carimbos en sus fiestas, español era su lengua,
    le ponían ritmo en bomba, a castañuelas de españa vieja.

    se queda allí, se queda allí, se queda allí, es mi raíz.

    betances abrió los pasos, los negros son ciudadanos,
    esa noche tocaron bomba, para la danza puertorriqueña.

    se queda allí, se queda allí, se queda allí, es mi raíz.

    la bomba ya está mezclada con las rimas jibareñas,
    hundida ella se encontraba, bailando plena borinquen tierra.

    se queda allí, se queda allí, se queda allí, es mi raíz.

    me hace cantar, me hace reír,
    me pone contento, me siento feliz.

    se queda allí, se queda allí, se queda allí, es mi raíz.

música, cultura popular

por el frío yo la canto, por los parques caminando,
siento el calor en mi cuerpo, mis huesos en clave,
me dan aliento.

se queda allí, se queda allí, se queda allí, es mi raíz.

roberto lleva sus chornos, a la luna de roena,
el futuro está bien claro, la bomba es base,
no hay quien la mueva.

métele encima el jazz, el rock o fox trot inglesa,
la bomba se va debajo, ay virgen no hay quien la mueva,
piñones baila de ponce, mayagüez con su lero,
cortijo es el padre, curet es el cura, maelo la canta,
roberto lo jura, se queda allí, la bomba vive en mí,
se queda allí, yo soy feliz, se queda allí, allí, allí

and at the end of these songs,
in praise of many beats,
my heart can only say:
se queda allí.

*se queda raíz. Oti
en todo*

Mainstream Ethics
(ética corriente)

Americanización. Para el inglés

lady liberty

for liberty, your day filled in splendor,
july fourth, new york harbor, nineteen eighty-six,
midnight sky, fireworks splashing,
heaven exploding
into radiant bouquets,
wall street a backdrop of centennial adulation,
computerized capital angling cameras
celebrating the international symbol of freedom
stretched across micro-chips,
awacs surveillance,
wall-to-wall people, sailing ships,
gliding armies ferried
in pursuit of happiness, constitution adoration,
packaged television channels for liberty,
immigrant illusions
celebrated in the name of democratic principles,
god bless america, land of the star
spangled banner
that we love.

but the symbol suffered
one hundred years of decay
climbing up to the spined crown,
the fractured torch hand,
the ruptured intestines,
palms blistered and calloused,
feet embroidered in rust,
centennial decay,
the lady's eyes,
cataract filled, exposed
to sun and snow, a salty wind,
discolored verses staining her robe.

she needed re-molding, re-designing,
the decomposed body
now melted down for souvenirs,
lungs and limbs jailed

in scaffolding of ugly cubicles
incarcerating the body
as she prepared to receive
her twentieth-century transplant
paid for by pitching pennies,
hometown chicken barbecues,
marathons on america's main streets.
she heard the speeches:
the president's
the french and american partners,
the nation believed in her, rooted for the queen,
and lady liberty decided to reflect
on lincoln's emancipatory resoluteness,
on washington's patriotism,
on jefferson's lucidity,
on william jennings bryan's socialism,
on woodrow wilson's league of nations,
on roosevelt's new deal,
on kennedy's ecumenical postures,
and on martin luther king's non-violence.

lady liberty decided to reflect
on lillian wald's settlements,
on helen keller's sixth sense,
on susan b. anthony's suffrage movement,
on mother cabrini's giving soul,
on harriet tubman's stubborn pursuit of freedom.

just before she was touched,
just before she was dismantled,
lady liberty spoke,
she spoke for the principles,
for the preamble,
for the bill of rights,
and thirty-nine peaceful
presidential transitions,
and, just before she was touched,
lady liberty wanted to convey
her own resolutions,

her own bi-centennial goals,
so that in twenty eighty-six,
she would be smiling and she would be proud.
and then, just before she was touched,
and then, while she was being re-constructed,
and then, while she was being celebrated,
she spoke.

if you touch me, touch ALL of my people
who need attention and societal repair,
give the tired and the poor
the same attention, AMERICA,
touch us ALL with liberty,
touch us ALL with liberty.

hunger abounds, our soil is plentiful,
our technology advanced enough
to feed the world,
to feed humanity's hunger . . .
but let's celebrate not our wealth,
not our sophisticated defense,
not our scientific advancements,
not our intellectual adventures.
let us concentrate on our weaknesses,
on our societal needs,
for we will never be free
if indeed freedom is subjugated
to trampling upon people's needs.

this is a warning,
my beloved america.

so touch me,
and in touching me
touch all our people.
do not single me out,
touch all our people,
touch all our people,
all our people

            our people
                  people.

and then i shall truly enjoy
my day, filled in splendor,
july fourth, new york harbor,
nineteen eighty-six, midnight sky,
fireworks splashing,
heaven exploding
into radiant bouquets,
celebrating in the name of equality,
in the pursuit of happiness,
god bless america,
land of star
spangled banner
that we love.

bag lady

if god were to come
and not be noticed
what better place
than a cold fortress
castle naked street.

latero story
(*can pickers*)

i am a twentieth-century welfare recipient
moonlighting in the sun as a latero
a job invented by national and state laws
designed to re-cycle aluminum cans
to return to consumer acid laden
gastric inflammation pituitary glands
coca diet rite low-cal godsons
of artificially flavored malignant
indigestions somewhere down the line
of a cancerous cell

i collect from garbage cans in outdoor facilities
congested with putrid residues
my hands shelving themselves
opening plastic bags never knowing
what to encounter

several times a day i touch evil rituals
slit throats of chickens
tongues of poisoned rats
salivating on my index finger
smells of month old rotten food
next to pamper's diarrhea
dry blood infectious diseases
hypodermic needles tissued with
heroine water drops pilfered in
slimy grease blood hazardous waste materials
but I cannot use rubber gloves
they undermine my daily profit

i am a twentieth-century welfare recipient
moonlighting during the day as a latero
making it big in america
someday i might become experienced enough
to offer technical assistance
to other lateros

i am thinking of publishing
my own guide to latero collecting
and founding a latero's union to offer
medical dental benefits

i am a twentieth-century welfare recipient
moonlighting at night as a latero
i am considered some kind of expert
at collecting cans during fifth avenue parades
i can now hire workers at twenty
five cents an hour guaranteed salary
and fifty per cent of two and one half cents
profit on each can collected
i am a twentieth-century welfare recipient
moonlighting at midnight as a latero
i am becoming an entrepreneur
an american success story
i have hired bag ladies to keep peddlers
from my territories
i have read in some guide to success
that in order to get rich
to make it big
i have to sacrifice myself
moonlighting until dawn by digging
deeper into the extra can margin of profit
i am on my way up the opportunistic
ladder of success
in ten years i will quit welfare
to become a legitimate businessman
i'll soon become a latero executive
with corporate conglomerate intents
god bless america.

drink

what
the
hell,
you
lovely
loneliness,
embrace
me
once
again!

preacher

god bless sister sarah
she dreamt of jesus
drinking a glass of water with her
and said sister sarah that she woke up
and we all know sister sarah's struggles
yes, the lord comes down in strange ways
praise the lord, alleluia
gloria a dios for our puerto rican congregation!
there's a message for sister sarah
and to all of you sinners of the bottle
don't let the evil ways of satan
drive you down the gypsy road
invite you to the wine cooler bedroom of the devil
do not be tempted
for jesus came to sister sarah
to bring down a message, brothers and sisters
to get high, yes, high with the lord
to get stoned, yes, stoned with the almighty
to get blasted, yes, blasted with the savior
to get intoxicated, yes, intoxicated with jesus
praise the lord, alleluia
gloria a dios for our spanish-speaking congregation!
nothing is more enlightening
than to drink the life of jesus
one water drink, is all you need
one drink, to see the after world
one drink, to feeeel goooooood inside
one drink, brothers and sisters
alleluia, praise the lord
gloria a dios for our nuyorican congregation!
pick up the pages of the bible
and get yourself drunk
all the way up to salvation
thumbs up to that sweet
wine taste of jesus, yes sir
let us raise our chalices to the lord's words
yes sir, alleluia

let's gobble up the champagne toast of salvation
yes sir, alleluia
drink jesus, we say yes
drink jesus, we say yes
drink jesus, we all say yes
jesus is the road
to eternal freedom
come, everyone,
together, let's say
alleluia, gloria a dios!

newscaster

some crazy white anglo saxon yale-educated
speechwriter got high on some french acid dope
in an international conference of the non-aligned
meeting with the western powers . . .
the president wanted a "liberation speech"
to compete with mitter and
to obtain a new base agreement from felipe gonzález
and to upstage castro's inflammatory anti-american
anti-imperialistic speech . . .

the writer, high on mescaline,
devised a wasp proposal
which made the u.s. and the president
sound extremely visionary . . .
the president announced that puerto rico
would be given independence
as a new democratic model . . .

the speech received wonderful praises
the president immediately conferred
with the non-aligned for new military bases . . .
the president encouraged the speechwriter
to draft a "detailed plan"
the writer got some more mescaline
and devised a method for the american-japanese
industrial complex to make "puerto rico
a third-world economic training base"
for manufacturing mini-parts for computers.

the short range idea ran into trouble
the pentagon and the joint military council
pressured the defense secretary
to retain the puerto rican commonwealth
"why rock the boat?"
"we need puerto rico to monitor the cubans"
"the island is a secret training center for
freedom fighters crushing marxism in latin america."

the president blamed the speechwriter
the speechwriter claimed that some crazy
puerto-rican-on-the-run-terrorist
had given him a leftist pill
that drove him insane
and into becoming a temporary agent
for the socialist cause . . .
the president rescinded his original independence plan . . .

colonialism speeches were the five-course highlights
during the evening supper meal.

hate

watch
out

for
the
venom

of
its
first
bite.

guerrilla

if it were not for european colonizers, spanish caudillos
sailing to romantic adventures on the high seas,
exploring myths, conquering gold for the mother land,
stealing american riches, torturing indians,
imposing christianity, all in the name of god,
driving natives into the mountains,
possessing, re-naming, murdering, extorting
in the name of the queen

if it were not for the monroe doctrine
big stick intervention, gradual imperialistic
western domination of mexican-indian lands,
colonizing nations, rough riding into
latin america, remembering the maine,
interfering in caribbean affairs,
entering puerto rico without an invitation,
sneaking into its southern borders,
buying governments for dictatorships
in the name of democracy,
at the expense of poor peasants
and broken banana republics . . .

if it were not for all of these injustices, then:

we would not have to pick up the gun
to humanize the puss-filled carcass
of your infectious terminal cancer . . .

we would not have to pick up the gun
to win over slimy landlords masturbating
on the hypocrisy of feudal promises,
stealing the wages of workers who
have toiled sixty hours on the blistering
face of the sun to find out on payroll lines
that the stinking food and the homeless shelter
was all their weekly checks would buy,

your laughing faces taking advantage
of simple humanity.

we would not have to pick up the gun,
to pulverize your bodies into evil dust,
to burn your skulls, to mame your legs,
to cut your throat, to feed it to the vultures,
to capture your after-spirit,
to rape your soul with evil rituals,
to exterminate and extinguish you with bullets,
to dispose of you in the stinking pool
in which we deposit our wastes
on the day of our victory meal,
when we free ourselves
from your corporate domination,
when we use your mouth openly suspended
to receive the toilet of our hatred.

that's how far your murdering cancer has spread.

there is no turning back,
very little room for negotiations,
there is no compromising.
you are destined not to win
anywhere in the world.
we are the antidote,
we are guided
by universal love
to destroy you

friend

we came
to hate
each other.

we became
bitter
enemies.

even then
i trusted
that
i trusted
you.

handshake

flesh
leaves

finger
tree
branches

palm
roots
clinched

two
nations
blood
pumping
adrenaline
reaching out
exploring
mutuality

poet

endlessly
chronological
wordsmith
underprivileged
sub-vulgate
penniless
moribund
marching
constantly
defying
endlessly
the last is first
the last is the base
chiselers
of letters
relentless
adventurers
endlessly . . .

children

every
thing
ever
imagined
conceived
once
again!

melao

melao was nineteen years old
when he arrived from santurce
spanish-speaking streets

melao is thirty-nine years old
in new york still speaking
santurce spanish streets

melaíto his son now answered
in black american soul english talk
with native plena sounds
and primitive urban salsa beats

somehow melao was not concerned
at the neighborly criticism
of his son's disparate sounding
talk

melao remembered he was criticized
back in puerto rico for speaking
arrabal black spanish
in the required english class

melao knew that if anybody
called his son american
they would shout puertorro
in english and spanish
meaning i am puerto rican
coming from yo soy boricua
i am a jíbaro
dual mixtures of melao and melaíto's
spanglish-speaking son
así es la cosa papá

viejo

sí, yes, es verdad, we cannot
run too fast anymore,
but we know that if a thief
overtakes us,
at any street corner,
we will not allow ourselves
to be touched.
we will talk mildly
to the assailant.
we will hand over to
the sinvergüenza
everything in our possession
and, if we're walking with a lady,
we will calm all our emotions
bien tranquilito, "take it all,
you can have it, just don't hurt the lady,
do anything you want to me,
we will turn our backs,
walk in the middle of the street,
without any trouble, go in peace,
take it all."

good. he took it all,
but he left me intact,
but i know he lives in the neighborhood.
the network of our bodega, barbería, bakeries
will identify el canalla.
my grandson fights karate,
he went out looking for el canalla's heart
to deliver it to his mother,
i told him it was my business.

so everybody
can rest assured
that any moment now
his groins

will be ground
as basement
appetizer
for
alley
cats.
verdad, socio?

machista

la, tú sabes, tipa esa, me tiene, lo oíste,
la mente, tú sabes, tumbao, con su ritmo caliente,
el estado mío mental está, ajá, eso mismo,
y ella dice, que todavía no le he hecho nada,
brother, me dijo que yo tenía
que coger un training de resistencia,
me lavó la cabeza, me maniobró, me enchutó.

brother, y yo que creía que era el máximo exponente,
graduado con doctorado de la universidad de bembas
con una maestría en labios y un bachi yo-no-sé-qué
rato en lenguas, yo creía que nadie podría
comerme mi coco cerebral, que estaba en control
supremo de mis acciones.

óyeme, brother, la tú sabes, tipa esa, malvada,
semi-y-qué-hembra, jíbara, urbana,
calurosa de su andar, black y qué
english morena, callejera, professional,
buena hija de arroz y habichuelas,
rumbera y qué progressive dancer type,
me salió, y que detrás pa' lante,
en plena esquina, brother, me amedrentó,
diciéndome con sus manos en sus hips,
en inglés y en español y que:

> "look here, brother, you cannot control me,
> so, don't even try, i have too many options
> to be convinced by your guajiro
> back-dated menaces or your semi-jealousies,
> whatever you say, i am not buying macho talk."

brother, y entonces yo le alcé mi lengua,
como para agarrarla, para atraparla, y pa' qué
fue eso, se puso más prieta, se le salió lo negro:

"who do you think you are?
i am living my life at the moment,
i am not gonna hang around you,
i don't need you,
you better be on the ball, all the time,
o si no, tú estás caliente with my boredom,
y si te da la gana de irte, i'm not going
to exprimir ni una lágrima, not even one tear,
honey, i got too much on the ball,
and i work too hard to sit down
at seven o'clock and worry about
your dull inactivities, tipo,

ya tú sabes, ponte en algo."

brother, la tipa se fue, tú sabes, enfogoná . . .
brother, pero yo soy el machito,
y esta noche, yo pensé, esta noche yo
la voy a endulzar, a atraparla,
yo sé lo que a ella le gusta,
o lo que le va a gustar,
brother, y no te malentiendas,
yo la quiero, en serio,
with my daily brainstorming,
yo le rapeo hasta en english,
brother, hoy perdí la batalla,
pero i am not gonna lose the war.

brother, entonces, la llamé
to take her out,
come, as friends, tonight,
dijo, "yes," brother,

la tipa esa me dejó en la puerta,
al lado del doorman
sin subir con ella en el elevador,
después que yo gasté cien cohetes,
tuve que andar siete bloques al subway.

i was broke, pelao, y la tipa se ofreció
a pagar la mitad, pero yo insistí en pagarlo todo,
y ahora, solo, en el subway,
at three o'clock in the morning,
perdona que te llame tan tarde, brother,
pero hay y que un delay,
y ella durmiendo en su cama,
and i just called her to go over,
y la tipa esa me dijo que mañana
me mandaba un money order for fifty dollars,
porque ella estaba cansada de mí
"boring, non-progressive, out of style
language talk, therefore i am gonna
change my phone,"
yo le contesté, "out of style?
qué diablo es eso? i dress good."
y ella me contestó que con mi
"ignorancia estás jodío."
me enganchó el teléfono,
óyeme, brother, yo creo que la tipa
esa está loca,
y no viene el subway.

compañero

Habla mujer

te digo, i tell you, compañero, mírame bien,
look at what you see, lo que soy, what I am,
te digo, i tell you, compañero, mírame bien,
i am not looking for the moment, compañero,
i am not looking for a fly-by-night relationship,
i am looking to grow, to be independent,
to be assertive, to educate myself,
i am looking for equality, on all levels, personal,
family, societal, i am looking for comprehension,
for tranquility, for dialogue,
i am looking to survive the ups and downs,
without humiliation, so think twice, compañero,
before you think about our future happiness,
you must understand what i am, compañero,
don't underestimate me,
don't crowd me,
don't exploit me,
it is your responsibility, tu responsabilidad,
to respect me, compañero,
and if you do, the treasures of my ultimate desires
will be nurturing you constantemente,
to make you a stronger man
as you make me a stronger woman.
i'll give you everything, everything,
i'll give you todo, all, compañero,
i'll give you the universe,
secretly for your private moments,
and you will give me back
the same commitment so that
we will never suffer from an
unemotional and cold goodbye.
i love you,
compañero.

titi
(*to Evelina López Antonetty*)

Simplicity stares silently stares silently
Silently silently simplicty stares silently
Stubbornly simplicty stares silently
Silenciosamente:

> We come to seize your breath
> We come to seize your formality
> Nation of nephews-nieces
> Community of confidants-poets-politicians
> City of educators-lawyers-students-activists
> Town of mothers-fathers-sisters-brothers
> Pueblo of brotherhood-sisterhood
> Stronger than ever; smarter than ever
> Generations of godsons-grandsons-great
> Granddaughters-grandfathers-abuelas
> We come to touch you, Titi:

Madrina-Madama-Warrior-Congregation-Talent-Commitment
Determined to fight injustices, oppression
Determined to confront systems, constantly
Unending-unyielding spiritual/physical devotion:

> A BELL LENA-VOICE
> A BELL LEAN-GRACEFUL
> A BELL ELITE
> A BELL MUSICAL SOUNDS
> A BELL POWER-RESPECT
> A BELL DEDICATION
> EVELINA-EVELINA:

We march, soldiers of your commitments
We will fill the vacuum-void-vulnerability
Of-your absence we-will-cross-communicate
To-each-other-and-you-Titi—will-monitor-our
Calls-you-Titi-will-embrace-our-freedom
To-win-to-grow-Titi-you-will-spread-our wings

MAESTRA, how beautifully you taught us:

Titi-testament tu OBRA
Tan linda tu OBRA tan
Linda tu OBRA tan pura
Como Salinas llena de ORO
TU MIRADA.

Te necesitamos, always
Protégenos siempre, always
Regáñanos cariñosamente, always
Keep us on your ALERT, always, always
We will march to give you

EL BESO, Titi,
EL BESO, Titi,
EL BESO DE TU INTEGRIDAD

Gracias por tus tantas contribuciones
Gracias for all of you that's yet to come
For you, Titi, we offer our HEARTS
Siempre, always, hasta siempre, BENDICIÓN
Compañera.

bochinche bilingüe

los únicos que tienen
problemas con el vernáculo
lingüístico diario de nuestra gente
cuando habla de
las experiencias de su cultura popular
son los que estudian solamente
a través de los libros
porque no tienen tiempo para
hablar a nadie, ya que se pasan
analizando y categorizando
la lengua exclusivamente
sin practicar el lenguaje.

el resto de estos
boring people
son extremistas aburridos
educadores perfumados
consumidores intelectuales
de la lengua clásica castellana
al nivel del siglo dieciocho
racistas monolingües en inglés
monolingües comemierdas en español
filósofos nihilistas
y revolucionarios mal entendidos
todos los cuales comparten
una gran pendejá
minoría.

migración

"en mi viejo san juan," calavera cantaba
sus dedos clavados en invierno, fría noche,
dos de la mañana, sentado en los stoops
de un edificio abandonado, suplicándole
sonidos a su guitarra,
pero:

        sus cuerdas no sonaban,
        el frío hacía daño,
        noel estrada, compositor,
        había muerto, un trovador
        callejero le lloraba:

"cuántos sueños forgé," calavera voz arrastrándose,
notas musicales, hondas huellas digitales,
guindando sobre cuerdas, sacándole música al hielo,
la fría tempestad,
creando verano con lágrimas,
calor de llantos,
"en mis noches de infancia, mi primera ilusión,"
sentado en los stoops,
"son recuerdos del alma,"
de un edificio abandonado,
pero:

        sus cuerdas no sonaban,
        el frío hacía daño,
        noel estrada, compositor,
        había muerto, un trovador
        callejero le lloraba:

"una tarde partí," calavera pensó en la decisión,
operation bootstrap, carreta, barco/avión,
"hacia extraña nación,"
sentado en los stoops,
"pues lo quiso el destino,"
de un edificio abandonado
pero:

sus cuerdas no sonaban,
el frío hacía daño,
noel estrada había muerto,
un trovador callejero
le lloraba:

"pero mi corazón," calavera pensó en el sueño,
de cualquier migrante hispano,
nadie quería morirse en américa,
"se quedó junto al mar,"
calavera plena melancolía,
el puertorro no se paró en ellis island,
se sentían short-range citizens,

venimos para regresar,
solamente nos quedamos
sentados en los stoops
porque el sueño se pudrió,
en la ilusión de los huecos
de un edificio abandonado,
pero:
                    sus cuerdas no sonaban,
                    el frío hacía daño,
                    noel estrada, había muerto,
                    un trovador callejero
                    le lloraba:

"pero el tiempo pasó," calavera cantó,
"y el destino," agrio licor
se le olvidó una estrofa,
"mi terrible nostalgia," la gran canción
coros en barberías,
"y no pude volver,"
muchedumbre night club celebraba,
"al san juan que yo amé,"
voces dulces alejadas de borinquen,
"pedacito de patria,"
calavera miró oscuridad,
"mi cabello blanqueó,"

oscuridad miró a calavera,
"ya mi vida se va,"
botella terminada,
"ya la muerte me llama,"
sentado en los stoops,
"y no puedo vivir,"
de un edificio abandonado,
"alejado de ti,"
calavera se paró, decidido,
"puerto rico del alma,"
calavera cantaba:

"adiós," andando hacia el east river,
"adiós," a batallar inconveniencias,
"adiós," a crear ritmos,
"borinquen," ganarle a la fría noche,
"querida," a esperar la madrugada,
"tierra," a apagar la luna,
"de mi amor," esperando el sol,
"adiós," caliente calor,
"adiós," calavera lloraba,
"adiós," sus lágrimas,
"mi diosa," calientes,
"del mar," bajando hasta el suelo,
"mi reina," quemando la acera, carretera,
"del palmar," lágrimas en transcurso,
"me voy," aclimaban las cuerdas,
"ya me voy," y pasaron por sus manos,
"pero un día," y todo se calentó,
"volveré," sin el sol,
"a buscar," y finalmente
"mi querer," las cuerdas sonaron,
"a soñar otra vez," el frío no hacía daño,
"en mi viejo," el sol salió, besó a calavera,
"san juan," al nombre de noel estrada.

calavera abrió las manos en un ritual
hacia el sol, calavera contestó, cantó, terminó,
"en mi viejo san juan."

barrio
(forenglishonly)

el inglés
se desforma
con el
calor de
tu cultura

lenguas en
sonidos
coloquiales
onomatopeyándose
con
aztlán
clave
del coquí

aquí
el español
se coge
a pecho
valorizado
profundamente

entonces
se
digestionan
anglicismos
nuyorriqueños
chicanerías
mezcladas
en spanish
idioms
dentro del
no-mare-wha
india
wha-re-monton

pitando
piropos
atoloquedá

entonces
es
que
surge
el
inglés
puro
"what's
happening
man,"
in
black
english

social club

un "trago straight," cuba libre de don q
y el speech que dice John F. Kennedy balanceado
con el alcalde de ponce, un indio
fumando la pipa, cara pintada colorá,
cuatro cigarros, pote de miel,
museo de reliquias, silla antropológica,
valores folklóricos, barrio urbano,
club fraternal, a nivel de esquina,
en oro plástico, allá arriba velando
san lázaro, su piel chillando
sangre sobre muletas, vellones y chavitos,
por la gracia de yemayá,
se estudian las costumbres,
que son la base del pueblo,
filosofía diaria, narración documentada.

la india en la vitrina, protege la puerta,
velas en escapularios de cocos,
congo haitiano, escultura de madera,
alcanzando a dos mujeres rubias,
con senos apropiados,
pero la negra africana,
guillada en incandescente,
es el afro-centro de la pared boricua,
sentada encima del tite, orgullosa
de su semi-desnuda realidad.

por la entrada del "capicu," "chucha,"
"dóblese hombre," "no me cierre la puerta,"
juego del dominó, al lado del billar,
Martin Luther King Jr. y Roberto Clemente,
observando los mitos, historias locales,
detalles de periódicos, en esta comunidad,
botellas de miller high life,
aguantan antenas, la vellonera es *out of order*,
hoy se usa "el music box,"
se venden cervecitas por camuflaje,

en tres esquinas, el sóngoro consongo de mamey,
hector lavoe gratis, para el deleite
de los pedro navajas, que venden escobas,
hechas de varas para pescar en los alcantarillados.

en la entrada del toilet
pusieron un tigre,
con la boca abierta,
y una pistola para advertirte,
que si entras a meterte estofá,
te va a comer un alacrán,
una persona inside solamente,
encima de canelones bilingües
encima, las películas de buck jones, humphrey
bogart, black cat, two-fisted jorge
negrete, revoluces de boca, a cada instante,
sólo quedan maones irregulares,
extra large, los viejos comentan,
que sus "barrigas de budweiser,"
no han llegado a ese extremo.

la bandera americana es solamente un suvenir,
trofeos con palabras mal deletreadas,
vírgenes suplicándole a los machos alzando pesas, dientes de
hierro protegen el retrato de
Rafael Cortijo, el más alto, una escultura de tiza,
en honor a nuestra música,
con la bandera de Puerto Rico,
en escudo de bomba.

el establecimiento rodeado
por cuatro cuadros,
hecho en gold plate,
por una muchacha que firma *md,*
la doctora de fresquerías,
que vende a quince pesos
escenas de tarzán
guindando de un árbol en la jungla,
desnudo con jane los dos *swinging*

en la misma soga pero jane cogió
el órgano de tarzán en vez de la soga,
tarzán con su cara dolorosa gritando,
"Jane, grab the goddamn vine, Jane!!"

en otro display las letras dicen,
EL GALLITO DE MANATI,
vemos un gallo grande,
de plumas negras,
con *psychedelic paint,*
y de momento debajo del gallo,
el órgano de macho más grande
y más pelao del pueblo,
ése es el gallo puertorro!

la muchacha que firma *md*
vende otro cuadro,
Ordenen sus Cerditos,
ahora in advance,
se ve un puerco
encima de una puerquita,
metiendo mano, también en
psychedelic holiday greetings,
dice el cuadro, "order your
christmas ham," the lechoncitos
"are being made to order,"
la puerquita contentita
sudando en "ecstasy!!"

Ismael Rivera hace los hombres soñar
las panderetas, número siete de
la suerte hoy, ocho por uno
tirando los topos, cincuenta cohetes
tragaos por la casa, paraíso de borinquen,
debajo de otra bandera de puerto rico,
y un retrato de don pedro albizu campos,
joven y nacionalista saliendo de la corte,
"defendiendo los derechos de mi patria,"

otra fría, pai, con rumba de Tito Rodríguez,
al compás de una plena, el entra-sale
vendedores de sopa en lata,
cincuenta chavos pa la curita,
un moreno vende wholesale
marketa de lipsticks por diez dólares.

dos mujeres, trabajadoras de factoría,
entran cuidadosamente a tomarse unas cervecitas,
mientras dos machitos de la vieja guardia
empiezan la controversia de panzas,
"tú eres una nenita al lado de mi falda,"
"cállate zafao,"
"tú hablas como el sapo,"
"vete a trabajar pa que me mantengas,"
"tú eres tan flaco que no le haces cosquilla
a un mapo,"
"anda como un gallo desenfrenao,"
a ver si las trabajadoras le ríen las gracias,
para empezar un rapeo.

observamos el tercer retrato de John F. Kennedy,
con su hermano Robert F. Kennedy,
artículo de periódico
con el retrato de Marilyn Monroe,
acusando que Robert sirvió de mensajero
al presidente para tirarle piropos
a Marilyn, mientras Jacqueline estaba
encinta de Caroline. El Papa Juan
veinte y tres bendice todo esto con
la señal de la cruz.

la doctora de fresquerías,
la *md*, que hace los cuadros,
la arrestaron por ser terrorista,
nadie lo cree, cómo es posible,
finalmente se llega a la conclusión que,
como ella era "de la underground,"
tenía que hacer "un trabajo,"

"totalmente absurdo,"
para que "no la descubrieran,"
era como los nacionalistas
que vinieron a nueva york
fugándose en los cincuentas,
y se volvieron ministros pentecostales.

los hombres se acercan cuidadosamente
estudiando el último cuadro de la *md,*
al *road runner* lo están ahorcando
por el *coyote*, que siempre lo persigue,
con la manguera pelá del órgano,
penetrándose en la letra *psychedelic* del coyote,
"now 'Beep Beep,' you sanafabeech,"
los hombres diciendo que los cuadros
"son collector's items,"
el dueño comentando que quizás
"había un tema revolucionario
adentro de toda esa fresquería,"
en el social club,
museo de reliquias,
silla antropológica,
valores folklóricos
de un barrio urbano,
club fraternal,
a nivel de esquina,
filosofía diaria,
narración documentada.

hispano

un
vals
en
vallenato
picoteando
samba
merengueada
con
ranchera
de
mambo
combinada
en
salsa
de
plena
polka
rumbeando
bolero
a
la
cha
cha
cha
chi
cha
peruana
cumbia
folklórica
bomba
y
guaracha
picaíta
seis
de
andino
danza

mezclada
en
baladas
nocturnas
de
tango
son
de
unotodos
todosuno
pasitos
unidos
a la
vuelta
del
compás.

conciencia

te hablo porque puedo hablar
tengo la confianza que entiendes
mi genocidio mi pesadilla
mi esclavitud mis cadenas invisibles
mis libertades falsas
te digo que nuestra gente duerme

te hablo porque puedo hablar
porque no somos uno tú y yo
porque no estamos unidos tú y yo
porque no buscamos la expresión interna

te hablo y ahora te pregunto

    de qué manera podemos acercarnos mutuamente
    que es el todo-feliz que anhelamos
    con qué intención existe el pensamiento
    cuál verso en la soledad decimos dormimos vivimos

te pregunto y te contesto
no existe tal fenómeno
la sociedad ha roto tal camino
sólo se encuentran
frases mutiladas
sílabas congeladas
silencio desorientado
brisa volando locamente
no existe
un compañerismo acogedor
un momento colectivo para entonarnos
calentarnos porque así es la ley
natural de los sentidos

te hablo porque puedo hablar
porque te busco ansiosamente
por las avenidas del arrabal
abajo en mil angustias

oigo algo que hay
algo que nos hace pensar que hay
algo que impide a lumbre de regocijos que hay
algo que nos achanta el progreso
te pregunto porque entiendo
que tú sigues buscando
dentro de mil pellejos
dentro de la nada del silencio
dentro de agrios momentos
allá en el abajo-biznieto-sufrimiento
muchas veces concluimos que
nada somos ni seremos
somos esclavos del dulce caminar de la pobreza
cadena perpetua
calle sin salida
dolores familiares
decepciones
pesadillas de amores pisoteados
arrogante pecado competencia
ilusiones de trabajo,
el landlord todo-lo-nuestro rata malo
a veces nos apesta
el sudor de los esfuerzos
sacamos lengua al zalapastroso negociante
maldecimos al dichoso olor del progreso
penetrándose como si hubiera futuro
y nosotros fiel compradores
planeando la vida del carrusel
comiendo el mango agrio de ilusiones
la cáscara podrida carcajada del progreso
hasta aquí llegan las llagas de la búsqueda
a ver si cerramos los ojos
tan siquiera un momento
a ver si

        un nosotros
        un nosotros verdadero
        un nosotros poderoso
        un nosotros lleno
        un nosotros amoroso

a ver si
un nosotros humano
alzamos las voces
constantemente
al ritmo de insistencia
resistencia
un nosotros crítico
que abre la boca
que no se estanca
un nosotros que declara
somos el mar de nuestro destino
somos la lengua de nuestras acciones
no le tememos al miedo
sabemos que el sin hablar nos oprime
que caiga lo que caiga como caiga
cuando caiga que caiga donde caiga
el silencio nos mata aquí
inundémonos con la mirada fija
con la pelea externa
pónganse ciegos
no oigan la soledad
háganse soldados de su destino
sin parar
cuando pierdas párate
sin parar
habla otra vez
caíste párate
esta fuerza en que vivimos
sólo conoce
sólo reconoce

       la demanda
       la huelga
       el motín
       la violencia
       la persistencia
       la política electoral
       el dinero

la lengua es
la ametralladora
de la libertad
háganlo para el futuro
de nuestros hijos
oigan no se achanten
ganaremos.

AmeRican

Ethnic Tributes

book
(to all poets, all of us)

the day arrived,
published book date,
calling mamá to
collect blessings
roots, inside
nicolás kanellos
writing room,
he opens a spanish
literature bookcase . . .
the smell of all that
history, the moisture
aging scent of relics:
the bible, cervantes,
shakespeare, jefferson,
lope de vega, brecht,
unamuno, nietzche,
neruda, hemingway,
pietri, toast to
him, greeting him
giving him
sacred space, and now,
feast: the mexican
singer marco antonio
muñíz, honors him
with puerto rican
composer rafael hernández's
morning medley melodies . . .
meditating, the book
caught itself in the
macho of the "urbane,"
the virgin first copy,
just touched the author's
nervously expressive
trembling hands and,
looking from the inner
sanctum of his eyes,

he opened me, fingers
gently upon my covers,
. . . sanctifying
feeling of accomplishment
beatified my total self,
and, in a quiet breath
of aspiration, i looked upon
the him and the her reflections,
found on the first page
of a new book and i
allowed myself to call me
beautiful

intellectual

so historically total
so minutely precise
so accurately detailed
so politically active
so grammatically arrogant
so academically prepared
so literally perfect
so ethnically snobbish
so aristocratically professional
so if you want to challenge me,
be prepared to lose the argument,
for i am too humanly infallible
about my researched assertions,
so take it or leave it,
the latter is your wisest choice,
do not arouse my anger,
i will reduce you to a
bibliographical ibidem,
demoting you to childhood,
in other words,
come out to kill,
and be dead
from the start.

boricua

we are a people
who love to love
we are loving
lovers who love
to love respect,
the best intentions
of friendship,
and we judge
from the moment on, no
matter who you are,
and, if we find
sincere smiles,
we can be friends,
and, if we have a
drink together,
we can be brothers,
on the spot, no
matter who you are,
and we have a lot
of black & white
& yellow & red
people whom we
befriend, we're
ready to love
with you, that's
why we
say, let there
be no prejudice,
on race, color is
generally color-blind
with us, that's our
contribution, all
the colors are tied
to our one,
but we must fight
the bad intentions,
we must respect

each other's values,
but guess what,
we're not the only ones,
and we offer what your
love has taught us,
and what you're worth
in our self-respect,
we are a people
who love to love
who are loving
lovers who love
to love respect.

arab

allah be praised
allah almighty
allah allah
allah be praised
protect us
allah the highest
all-knowing
all-merciful
all-faithful
allah, you come to us,
allah be praised, we will protect your laws,
allah be praised, we will protect your lands,
allah be praised, we will protect your name,
allah be praised, we will protect your name,
allah, we will protect ourselves,
allah, we will protect ourselves,
allah, we will protect your name,
allah, our hands are in your will,
allah, your will, allah, we're blinded,
    your will, allah, our will,
        allah, my will,
        allah, i will fight,
        allah, until we win,
        allah, until we win,
        allah, we win we win,
           we win we win,
           win we win,
             we win,
               in
            aaaaaaaaaaaaaaaaa
            llaaaaaaaaaaaaaah
            victory,
            your
            name!

black

full moonlight in central park
metropolitan house: la boheme
a soprano voice reaching
thirty thousand people sitting in
summer evening, the trumpets
sang, their winds circulating,
integrating and, there were
blacks who had suffered,
blacks who had been slaves,
blacks who were now chanting
to protect world interests,
african, caribbean, urban european,
black madame, a la leontyne price,
cabling the world into classical
aesthetic leadership,
its humanity,
its humanity,
a testament
to all who
over
come
song,
song,
song!

chinese

all
those
fa
ces
hap
py
el
ders
trea
ted
with
res
pect
by
the
clan
won
der
ful
chi
nese
cul
ture
all
pay
ing
hom
age
to
the
wise

cuban

(*for nicolás guillén*)

base prieta jerigonza
(escondida en lo cristiano)
huracán secreto
luna llena se desvela
se desborda:
    ¡bajó el cielo, maraña gloriosa!
    ¡bajó el cielo, espíritu espanto!
    ¡bajó el cielo, guaguancó de mambo!
    ¡estrellas en coro, salen nicollenando!
base prieta jerigonza
(escondida en lo cristiano)
huracán secreto
luna llena se desvela
se desborda, sale OCHA
camino real, voz maravillosa:

    lo que vale es lo que vive en la conciencia,
    el que sabe de igualdad en su todo lo comenta,
    no hay quien embabuque al niche desengañado,
    en el secreto todo se guarda, todo se observa.

base prieta jerigonza
(escondida en lo cristiano)
huracán secreto
luna llena se revela
se desborda, se enamora:

    ¡se sabe que al dormir hay sueño
    prieto, ñañiguero, abacuado en ogunero
    changoteando madamas yorubistas
    adentro del sueño otro sueño
    yemayado de orishas
    sacudiendo caderas de europeo
    el origen se preserva

al vaivén de ideas claras
al vaivén de ideas claras
ideas claras caribeñas!

salió el sol, sus rayos atravesando
    rayos, largas piernas afriqueñas
    rayos, trompetas charanga europea
    rayos, tambores indígenas se encuentran
    rayos, rompiendo todo esclavo
    rayos, preservando colores de resguardo
    rayos, con los viejos africanos
    libremente exclamando:
    ¡somos los mismos, los mismos éramos
    y, aún más, un nuevo cambio:
    no somos ni negros, no somos ni africanos
    somos humanos, respaldándonos, somos humanos
    así, que salga el sol, así que siga la luna
    así, que salga el sol, así que siga la luna
    así, que suba el cielo, adiós al sueño
    yo le canto a la lumbre del glorioso despertar
    yo le canto a la lumbre del glorioso despertar!

english

so
exquisite
general
overtones
tonalities
transfused
transcending
growing
definitions
expansions
most-advanced
researching
ex-creating-out
clearest
clarity
orgasms
of
confusion
we-hate-love
your
forced
indulgences
our
backbones
constantly
searching
for-your-greatness
that
will
re-define
ambitions
in-your-language
we
struggle
to
make
everyone

humanistically
proud
of
your
relationship
to
the
growth
of
the
world

greek

looking to find modern mythology
in the descendants
of ancient playwrights, to see if
something rubbed off, was aristotle
brown in color, no, it couldn't be,
well, anyway, the new poets of god,
are making money, simply because the
poets were kept unemployed by some sleazy
characters throughout history,

where else could i find such
mythological realities, i wonder
if the greek scientists, who are
now board chairmen, were lighter in
skin than the playwrights, that
might explain the reason for their poets'
expulsion, no, it couldn't be . . .

well, anyway, i love all greeks,
and all the colors they may wish
to add to this poem, but i always
think they are puerto ricans,
that's why i only mythologize
in greek restaurants open
twenty-four hours a day
in new york.

irish
(*odes*)

march song

bobby	sands	irish	land
sands	irish	land	bobby
irish	land	bobby	sands
land	bobby	sands	irish
bobby	sands	irish	land

eulogy

warriors never die
never smile warriors
never smile never die
hear the cry
hear the cry
hear the cry
warriors never cry
smile warriors never
smile cry warriors
always smile cry
warriors always smile
cry always never cry
hear the cry smile
hear the smile cry
always always
hear the cry
patriotic smile

spirit

as i die i live
the earth purity
body without water
bread i cleansed
i bathed in irish
green fragrance

freely flowing
forever flag
fasting
freedom
fasting
ireland
ira-land
free ireland
free ireland
my gut of dignity
of trust of truth
of love i gave all
i gave all
to free ireland
to free ireland

italian
(*ballad*)

young dude
is old dude
is same dude
we grew dude
young dude
is old dude
is same dude
we grew dude
he sang blues
the old blues
the new blues
the top blues
youngsters were
old dudes old dudes
were young dudes
the lyrics distinguished
all decades agreed with
the crooner the loner
the proud style
the voice range
transcended
his lifetime
so always always sing
like blue eyes
young blue eyes
old blue eyes
same blue eyes
so always always sing
please, blue eyes.

jamaican

reach their guts into the caribbean
the second africa, divided by yemayá
reach their guts into the third world
marley-manley emerging people
reach their guts into urban america
reggae-reggae, modern english
reach their guts into ethiopia
rastafarian celebrated deities
reach their guts into washington square park
jamaican english, folkloric blackness
reach their guts into puerto ricans
where we shared everything for free
yeah, brother, very good, very, very
good, yeah, real good!

japanese
(*joke?*)

he was ten years old in 1942
when they killed mama-san
and papa-san (street vendors
in pearl harbor) the day on
the japanese attack, on
december 7th, he fled to
the mountains of a deserted
hawaiian island, way up there
near a volcano, he grew to
find peace, the fifties, the
sixties, the seventies, the
volcano was erupting, he came
down from the mountains when
he was fifty years old in 1982
he arrived at sea-level
he was prepared to die
and, guess what, he saw
the billboard toyota ads
and he thought the japanese
had won the war.

jewish

we stand the pain of time
we stand across the pain of time
we withstood the harshest pain of time
we know you know that:
we will never again be persecuted
we will never again be lynched
we will protect ourselves from the world
yiddish always! we have a lot of names
in many languages we will communicate
yiddish always! we have a lot of names
in many languages we will communicate
the elders all taught the second tongue
we might be spanish, french, german, americans
yiddish always, we all can speak one tongue
we have a lot of names, in many languages
we stand the pain of time
we stand across the pain of time
we withstood all the pain of time
and we live, side by side, in peaceful harmony
but never, never, again.

russian

she scraped the church floor
with fervent devotion she shined marble
climbing up to the lord's resurrection
looking down, the madonna selected
her altar boys and choir boys who
walked her home into her apartment
she seduced young virgins
she painted her own saintly cherubims
twelve and thirteen years old
playing with her slowly and fruitfully
the first time, but she wanted
the second time, right away, and
the young boys were overtaken by her
brutal strength passion so strong
that the seraphims collapsed out of
sheer exhaustion, and then
she devoured them totally
she taught them to be macho
she taught them to be men
she polished fourteen-carat chalices.

spanish

your language outlives your world power.
but the english could not force you to change
the folkloric flavorings of all your former colonies
makes your language a major north and south american
tongue.
the atoms could not eradicate your pride,
it was not your armada stubbornness
that ultimately preserved your language.
it was the nativeness of the spanish,
mixing with the indians and the blacks,
who joined hands together, to maintain your precious
tongue,
just like the arabs, who visited you for
eight hundred years, leaving the black
skin flowers of andalucía,
the flamenco still making beauty with your tongue.
it was the stubbornness of the elders,
refusing the gnp national economic language,
not learning english at the expense of
much poverty and suffering, yet we maintained
your presence, without your maternal support.
Spain, you must speak on behalf of your language,
we await your affirmation of what we have fought to preserve.
ESPAÑOL, one of my lenguas, part of my tongue,
i'm gonna fight for you, i love you, spanish,
i'm your humble son.

mundo-world

¡ahí viene, ahí viene!
no me queda más remedio,
vivo adentro de la primera milla,
entonces yo la voy a esperar
corriendo desesperado hacia
el centro de wall street
esperando a la prostituta
madamo del maldito TEN
que evaporizará mis espíritus,
reduciéndome a una teoría
matemática adentro del NINE
por los cincuenta canales
nervios electrónicos del EIGHT
se penetran los aparatos ovarios
del satélite capitalizando el SEVEN
en la computadora musical del SIX
QUE ME LLEVA DESESPERADO
hacia un rumbo sin destino
que me convierte iluminosamente
en un brujo amante del impacto FIVE
¡ahí viene, ahí viene!
yo, cerrando los ojos,
yo, rogando a lo indígena,
que me separe del miedo,
que salve a todos los niños del FOUR
corriendo desesperado hacia
el centro de Wall Street
esperando a la prostituta
madamo del maldito THREE
que me hundirá en la tierra,
la que dio a luz a los neutrones del TWO
la que quemará mi existencia con un vapor,
fuego, caliente, destructor, fuego,
metiéndose en las raíces naturales del ONE.
¡aquí viene, aquí viene!
el impacto que bombardeará
nuestras almas explotando las caderas del desarrollo,

ZERO
la tierra despidiéndose de la luna
besándola con un cantito de la NADA.
hacia el rumbo sin destino,
hacia el rumbo sin destino,
quién sabe lo que se puede hacer
para evitar el maldito compás
de esa bomba en plena nuclear,
de esa bomba en plena nuclear.

Values

I. Pueblo

café

dry
roasted
out
of
sun
café
crushed
café
grinded
boiled
"colao"
café
aroma
into
nostrils
fresh
caffeine
drugging
sleep
into
an
awake
café
smells
deep
breath
long
stretch
eyes
open
café
day
light
mmmm
café
sabor

boyhood

behind our puerto rican santurce
house on bella vista street
buried in the yard we found a coffin
jorgito and i kept the secret
for two weeks we gathered enough
courage sunday after dinner
we dug for it
we paced around it
we opened it with a car jack
we found a black and white
nationalist flag
we looked at each other
"let's unveil it,"
"yeah, let's go all the way,"
we uncovered the flag
we found an arsenal of
weapons underground
live ammunition
patria o muerte slogans
land or death
there was no other choice
we looked at each other
we closed the coffin
we buried it with soil
we kept the secret.

negrito

el negrito
vino a nueva york
vio milagros
en sus ojos
su tía le pidió
un abrazo y le dijo,
"no te juntes con
los prietos, negrito."
el negrito
se rascó los piojos
y le dijo,
"pero titi, pero titi,
los prietos son negritos."
su tía le agarró
la mano y le dijo,
"no te juntes con
los molletos, negrito".
el negrito
se miró sus manos
y le dijo,
"pero titi, pero titi,
así no es puerto rico."
su tía le pidió
un besito y le dijo,
"si los cocolos te molestan,
corres; si te agarran, baila.
hazme caso, hazme caso,
negrito."
el negrito
bajó la cabeza
nueva york lo saludó,
nueva york lo saludó,
y le dijo,
"confusión"
nueva york lo saludó
y le dijo,
"confusión."

abuelito

cuando
el
padre
regaña
al
hijo
el
hijo
baja
la
cabeza
y
no
se
atreve
a
responder.
lo
máximo
es
el
orgullo
y
el
respeto
de
ser
hombre.
la
mentira
es
el
ogro
del
opio.
siempre
se

pide
permiso
al
pasar
entre
dos
personas.
a
los
mayores
de
familia
se
les
pide
la
bendición.

jíbaro

end of spring harvest,
el jíbaro mathematically
working the sun's energies,
nurturing every fruit to
blossom perfectly,
singing about
earth, la tierra,
time after time, acre after acre,
year after year, the land provided.
end of spring harvest,
el jíbaro's guitar
on la carreta,
pulling, ploughing slowly
towards sunset,
towards la cena,
towards the afternoon breeze,
land, love, moon,
the lyrics emerged,
décimas in place,
the ever-present "lo le lo lai,"
and then, the song,
canción.

ay bendito

oh, oh. ¡ay virgen!
fíjese, oiga, fíjese,
ay, bendito.
pero, ¿qué se puede hacer?
nada, ¿verdad?
ave maría.
ah, sí. ah, sí, es así.
pues, oiga,
si es la verdad.
pero, ¿qué se puede hacer?
nada, ¿verdad?
fíjese, oiga, fíjese.
mire, mire.
oh, sí, ¡hombre!
oiga, así somos
tan buenos, ¿verdad?
bendito.
¡ay, madre!
¡ay, dios mío!
¡ay, dios santo!
¡me da una pena!
ay, si la vida es así, oiga.
pero, ¿qué se puede hacer?
nada, ¿verdad?
fíjese, oiga, fíjese.
oiga, fíjese.

del pueblo

todos somos puertorriqueños, olvídate,
hasta el fin, pero, si
los gallitos de manatí
se enfrentan con
los cangrejeros de santurce,
no se sorprendan si
los cangrejeros le cortan
el cuello a un gallo
al comienzo del juego profesional
y no se sorprendan si
los gallitos le mentan a
la madre o a la abuela del
primer cangrejo prieto
y no se sorprendan si
todos bebemos juntos
emborrachando las
carcajadas.

deporte

métele mano mátalo brother
con un bolo punch derecha
larga al costado empínale
los puños con un fuerte
izquierdazo left jab al hocico
de sus ojos apabúllalo con
cuatro uppercuts durísimos
está sentido no oigas la campana
no le des break dale al pómulo
derecha puñal en la espina
dorsal de su corazón apúntale
combinaciones right-left
gancho de izquierda manufacturado
en la tierra dale la paliza
del siglo con los codos aterrizando
en las mejillas para que se le
caigan los dientes del impacto
de un over right machete para
que le partas el puente de
la nariz en dos destrúyele
el cuerpo hasta que se le caigan
las manos y cuando él no pueda
más cuando esté ya agotado
de descarga tan grande échate
hacia atrás y castígalo con
un martillazo en plena boca
y déjalo muerto sin que el
oficial tenga que contar a diez.

pai

compa primo cabo
compa primo cabo
socio venga acá
no se vaya disgustao
le doy la plena razón
por sus acciones
recuérdese que usted
es el padre de su hija
tiene razón en defenderla
no se apure compa
lo hizo bien
el buen ejemplo empieza
con el pai
y yo le digo
que cuando usted se paró
a llamarle la atención
al canalla que humilló
a su hija y cuando él
le contestó estrujadamente
y cuando usted le metió
tremenda pescozá ya yo
tenía las manos en mis
bolsillos y lo que iba
a salir era el cañón
que usaron los guerrilleros
para ganar la guerra de
vietnam y estaba calientito
así que usted siempre
tranquilo y yo le aseguraré
su espalda porque usted
sabe que es mi compa, pai.

Values

II. Nuyoricans

three-way warning poem
(*for josé luis gonzález*)

1. *sin nombre*	2. *sin nombre the first*
en	ste
el	reo
fon	type
do	pu
del	er
nu	to
yo	rri
ri	que
can	ño
hay	sí
un	yes
pu	we
er	can
to	cut
rri	you
que	all
ño	in

pana

i was in jail, brother. jail, brother.
encarcelao, under, bro, allá adentro,
solo, alone, bro, all by myself,
even with another name; y ese tipo
that i barely knew long ago,
he claimed he and my brother
had changed my diapers and
that he had seen me grow up,
desde chiquito, bro, he made me laugh,
he knew my case was a bum rap,
he knew i could defend my black belt,
but i was from his neighborhood,
it was his duty, he felt, to protect,
and that night he became the malote,
he went cell by cell setting the law
that he would cut heads with his teeth,
as machete, if any harm came my way,
i was released, he was doing life,
i go see him once a month, religiously,
bro, i slide him some good jades,
and i don't care if i get caught,
you know why, bro, porque
ese tipo es mi pana.

graffiters

in the near
distant future
archaeologists
will find ancient
hieroglyphics
fossils under
ground on subway
steel columns
inside the tunnel
underneath east
river they found
artifacts resembling
modern taíno symbols
the archeologists
analyzed signatures
interpreted to read
"our imprint to the
future we graffiters
wanted to somehow
survive the nuclear
holocaust to be
remembered for
whatever else
emerged."

grafiteros

los oídos enchufados con cassettes estereofónicos
caminando como guerrilleros allá abajo haciendo
música silenciosa con la firma presidencial del
progreso adentro de las raíces eléctricas ellos
escriben las señales bilingües odiadas como basura
como vandalismo los muchachitos del bronx y de
cualquier bloque hispano se sientan en los stoops
a diseñar los planes militares para penetrarse en
los sistemas alcantarillados para entrar a las
venas del subway a imprimir como fósiles la civi-
lización que será descubierta en el futuro incierto
ellos saben cómo preservar sus firmas nos estudian
científicamente el imprimatur de querer pertenecer
la ansiedad de acertar presencia con anuncios
modernos para inmortalizarse los muchachitos de
brooklyn y de cualquier bloque hispano guerrilleros
del silencio velando el horario de los trenes
cuándo vienen cuándo regresan mientras terminan
sus murales allá adentro en el hierro estancado
para asegurarse de un puesto microscópico en otras
generaciones hasta se ponen caretas de mono dándole
el gran susto al conductor.

nuyorican

yo peleo por ti, puerto rico,   ¿sabes?
yo me defiendo por tu nombre,   ¿sabes?
entro a tu isla, me siento extraño, ¿sabes?
entro a buscar más y más,   ¿sabes?
    pero tú con tus calumnias,
    me niegas tu sonrisa,
    me siento mal, agallao,
    yo soy tu hijo,
    de una migración,
    pecado forzado,
    me mandaste a nacer nativo en otras tierras,
    por qué, porque éramos pobres, ¿verdad?
    porque tú querías vaciarte de tu gente pobre,
    ahora regreso, con un corazón boricua, y tú,
    me desprecias, me miras mal, me atacas mi hablar,
    mientras comes mcdonalds en discotecas americanas,
    y no pude bailar la salsa en san juan, la que yo
    bailo en mis barrios llenos de todas tus costumbres,
    así que, si tú no me quieres, pues yo tengo
    un puerto rico sabrosísimo en que buscar refugio
    en nueva york, y en muchos otros callejones
    que honran tu presencia, preservando todos
    tus valores, así que, por favor, no me
    hagas sufrir, ¿sabes?

asimilao

assimilated? qué assimilated,
brother, yo soy asimilao,
así mi la o sí es verdad
tengo un lado asimilao.
you see, they went deep . . . Ass
oh . . . they went deeper . . . SEE
oh, oh, . . . they went deeper . . . ME
but the sound LAO was too black
for LATED, LAO could not be
trans*lated,* assimilated,
no, asimilao, melao,
it became a black
spanish word but
we do have asimilados
perfumados and by the
last count even they
were becoming asimilao
how can it be analyzed
as american? así que se
chavaron
trataron
pero no
pudieron
con el AO
de la palabra
principal, denles gracias a los prietos
que cambiaron asimilado al popular asimilao.

antiguas teorías neurológicas de asimi-
lación.

criollo story

i was drunk, sunday morning
sitting at tompkins square park
i was drummed-all-night
hitting them cueros
while the people sang the coros
bomba, plena, guaguancó, even
boogie jazz baritone
and black-man-mean tyrone
brother-friend from the neighborhood
tyrone, the singing, the dancing
the mixing up with rum into vodka
lo que venga, bro, échalo pa' cá
tonight is to vacilar
jamaican liquors washed in
constant beers, imported
exported and of course
colt .45's pistoling into
the final killer, dry red
wine from some crazy punk
rocker brother i tell you that
i was drunk, farts galore
pigeons fled new york
the lower east side was on
civil alert, to tell you the
truth, i was dead drunk, brother-man
tyrone telling me, "brother,
you look so bad, that if you
were thunderbird wine, i would
not even drink a free sample."
i was so drunk i could not even laugh
and then salvation time
"for you, mira, mondongo"
i thought tyrone was goofing on me
"you look like a mondongo yourself"
"no, no, not you, mira, i mean, HUMERA,
for HUMERA, mondongo, bro, adela,

she opens at five o'clock, let's
eat some of that tripe."

we walked into adela's five-
thirty morning mountain smell
of madrugada simmering concrete
puerto rican new york radio JIT
cuatro-music, recordando a borinquen
songs made famous by don Santiago
Grevi, and the crushed plantains
bollitos rounded boricua matzo all
around cleaned vinaigrette tripe
and patitas de cerdo pig feet,
softened to a melted overblown
delicacy, brother, and i tell you that
down went the russian vodka
the alcohol disappeared with
bites of calabaza-pumpkin pieces
and the one hundred proof bacardí
was choked by un canto de yautía
tubers that were rooting the European
dry red wine into total decolonization
and the broth, brother, EL CALDO
condimented garlic onions
peppered with whole tomatoes
that were melted by the low
heat, ese caldo was woefully
seducing the jamaican liquors
into compatibility, and down
went the BORRACHERA, bro, and
without talking, i looked
across to tyrone's second
plate, i thanked my brother
with a smile, as we kissed
adela, and what the hell
we took the number six into
orchard beach, on section
three, and we blew the sun
as we had serenaded the moon.

craqueao

four and one half billion
years old we are i heard
we are the most advanced
human beings believe me
i read that they study us
in chemistry we come from
organic soup dna and dinosaurs
who died and then the flowers
gave air i don't know all
the details but brother
we came from the sea and
we adapted to the air
we were fish
éramos pescao bacalao
pregúntaselo a darwin
salimos del agua somos
familia de los reptiles y
las tortugas que no regresaron
al mar y después cuando
estábamos en tierra nosotros
éramos gorilas y monos yo
vine del chimpancé brother
entonces empezamos a hablar
"óyeme, y ¿dónde está el darwin ese?"
"darwin está muerto."
"¡seguro, y tú craqueao!"

esquina dude

i like and dislike, like the good
dislikes the bad in everything, bro
nothing is better than nothing, bro
i integrate what i like, i reject
what i don't like, bro, nothing of
the past that is present is sacred
everything changes, bro, anything
that remains the same is doomed to
die, stubbornness must cover all my
angles, bro, y te lo digo sincerely
my judgement, bro, mi juicio, bro, bro
bro, i tell you that life is based
on the moment, el momento will
catch up to you, bro, i always prepare
myself for the constant ever present
moment, bro, the past, the present, the
future has nothing to do with the moment, and
yes, there are times when i open my blade
to cut, bro, i hope you understand
sincerely, sinceramente, bro, that if i
wound you, you probably deserved it
but i'll take you to the hospital if
you're still alive, and i'll face the
charges, but if we face each other, bro
de cara a cara, from face to face
you will know that you deserved that moment
porque, everybody knows i don't cut
unless you were meant to be cut, bro
so, be careful what you learn from me
and be careful not to use it against me
i love you, tú sabes that i do, de corazón
bro, but i might have to kill you
bro, but i hope you survive to be
my enemy or my friend, i'll take
you alive, either way, that's the way i
think, bro, that's my ideology
you better respect it bro, chévere

right on, hey, you're cold, bro
don't worry, i will kiss you openly
on the baseball field, nobody will
mess with you, i know you understood
everything i said, i know you don't
need a bilingual dictionary, what i said
can cut into any language, this is about
your life, i know you play no games
i'm glad you paid me, bro, porque
cuentas claras conservan amistades
you know exactly what i mean, gracias.

coqueta

sa
bes
e
res
be
lla

  con
  tes

  tas

    "si
    gue

      mi
      ran
      do

        sue
        ños."

enchulá

unfortunately, my new loves are
short range, i tried many times
to be long range, pero, time and
time again, you know, me decepcionaban
ahora, acepto los amores short range
honey, y te digo que mis amores se
ponen celosos, qué vaina, yo ahora
liberándome, queriendo short range
y ahora, todos ellos me quieren, y qué
long range, te lo digo, cuando yo era
buena, tú sabes, lo que yo quiero decir
entonces, me trataban mal, qué chavienda
ahora no soy tan buena, y los tengo
controlao, los hombres son masoquistas
verdad, te lo juro, me siento liberada
pero, concho, el diablo aquel todavía
me tiene la vida enchulá.

m'ija

i've been dying to call you m'ija
to tell you that last night i was
celebrating nothing, nothing to do
no money, no dress, nobody, m'ija,
un tremendo down, life is hard, even
on my birthday, eso te ha pasao a ti
también, verdad, but then, it all
changed, mamá called, she cooked a
"comidita," and she sewed a "nueva
blusita," real nice, and she baked
my favorite "postre," and one of my
"padrinos" remembered and there
was an envelope waiting and of course
i could have called him, m'ija, and
he would have been kneeling at my
door, but my pride insisted on my
pride, anyway, my family had remembered
yo estaba "llenita" and mamá gave me a
big abrazo after i blew out the candles
and i said to myself, "the hell with
it," i'm gonna get me a sexy dress
even if i bite my nails tomorrow for
falling behind on all my payments
pero, m'ija, i bought a sexy dress
and i went to the corso knowing he
would find me there, but i was going
to boogie and dance so freely that
i saw the tension in his jealous eyes
and he came to me to disculparse
and i really wanted him, anyway, so
muchas luces y boleros y besitos
y besos, del resto, mi amiga, ya tú
sabes, nena, lo celebré bien chévere
bien, bien chévere, te lo puedo contar
a ti todo, para eso somos amigas.

brava

they kept on telling me
"tú eres disparatera"
they kept on telling me
"no se entiende"
they kept on telling me
"habla claro, speak spanish"
they kept on telling me
telling me, telling me
and so, the inevitable
my spanish arrived
"tú quieres que yo hable
en español" y le dije
all the spanish words
in the vocabulary, you
know which ones, las que
cortan, and then i proceeded
to bilingualize it, i know
yo sé that que you know
tú sabes que yo soy
that i am puertorriqueña in
english and there's nothing
you can do but to accept
it como yo soy sabrosa
proud ask any street corner
where pride is what you defend
go ahead, ask me, on any street-
corner that i am not puertorriqueña,
come dímelo aquí en mi cara
offend me, atrévete, a menos
que tú quieras que yo te meta
un tremendo bochinche de soplamoco
pezcozá that's gonna hurt you
in either language, así que
no me jodas mucho, y si me jodes
keep it to yourself, a menos
que te quieras arriesgar
y encuentres and you find

pues, que el cementerio
está lleno de desgracias
prematuras, ¿estás claro?
are you clear? the cemetery
is full of premature short-
comings.

boda

the boda gathering modeling a wide display
of mademoiselle bazaar's modern rentals
on a bright june saturday afternoon of
bochinches, money problems, late musicians
el fotógrafo getting non-contract requests
y el tremendo chisme, which one of the two
suegras will ride the limousine, la grande
con aire acondicionado, the best man is late
big lenguas are saying, "te lo dije que a
ése no se puede trostear, se llevó el oro al
ponchop para ponerle plata a los anillos"
la novia es presbiteriana, but the groom's
mother is a big shot in her catholic parish
and she's forcing a second ceremony, one of
the smallest damas está "prendía," her dress
is too long, and she was placed last in line
she swore to count nine fingers from this day
on, one for each month, to see if la novia
"había metido las patas," the gathering outside
the church "encontraron los trajes
bien lindos," but el borrachón commented that
"the tuxedos esos son cosas pa' los prietos"
the friend of one of the caballeros embarrassed
him as the caballero was kissing the hand of
the dama "del traje colorao," by saying
"take the tuxedo off, you have to return it
tomorrow," the boyfriend of another dama
caught her flirting with another caballero
the boyfriend came over, there were tensions
at the end of the line, the women with rollers
for la fiesta later clicked their cameras
wanting to be novias again, the processional
music began, the best man llegó, la novia
towards the altar marched, they reached the
two reverends, el novio's hand, a nervous

testament, the ceremony began y el papá
desembarcó un tremendo suspiro dándole
un beso al redentor, "gracias dios mío
que aguanté esta jodienda y llevé a mi hija hasta el
altar."

puertorriqueña

oh no te apures
yo te los saco
uno a uno
si es familia
lo que tú quieres
yo te lo doy
dos si tú te
quedas aquí conmigo
tres y cuatro
yo te los saco
cinco yo te daré
seis si tú te
quedas aquí conmigo
siete yo te daré
ocho si tú te
quedas aquí conmigo
pase lo que pase
oh no te apures
yo te los saco
siempre y cuando
lo
    tu
      yo
        sea
          to
            í
            to
              mío
                'tá
                  to'
                    bien
                      si
                        no
                          nin
                            gu
                              no

chorna

tembandumba, now an elder,
gracefully watched the time:
"tatarabuela" her son calling her
"tatarabuela" her grandson calling her
"tatarabuela" her great-grandson calling her
"tatarabuela" her great-great-grandson
       her fourth-generation was born, calling her
       all of us calling her today "tatarabuela!"

tembandumba, now an elder,
gracefully watched the time:

she was a tatarabuela . . . . fourth generation
she was bisabuela . . . . third generation
she was abuela . . . . second generation
she was madre . . . . first generation
she had them in two lands
she had them in spanish
she had them in english
she had them black and white
she had them duplicated with beautiful women.

tembandumba, now an elder,
gracefully watched the time:

"tatarabuela" her great-great grandson-tataranieto
       turned sixteen, the generations called
       him macho-macho, bear children, macho,
       her great great great grandson-chorno,
       her fifth-generation was born, calling her
       all of us calling her today "CHORNA!"
tembandumba, now an elder,
tembandumba, chorna, mulata construction
elegantly walking, shaking forever youthful,
time and time and time and time again!

Values

III. Rituals

thinking

muerte, el respirar suspira
muerte, careciendo lágrimas
muerte, tempestad infinita
muerte, tú tienes las llaves
muerte, tú tienes las llaves
del pensar que no conozco
por eso te espero
por eso te peleo
por eso te odio
muerte, tú tienes las llaves
y yo, como veo lo que siento
y yo, como siento lo que no veo
  yo, como siento lo que no veo
      como siento lo que no veo
          siento lo que no veo
             lo que no veo
               que no veo
                  no veo
                    veo
                       eo,
                       o o o u a e i o
                       siento
                       sonidos
                       así
                       que
                       vendré
                       regresaré
                       de nuevo
                       en
                       al
                       go

muerte, un perro
      se para
      me mira
      me mira
      lo siento
      se va andando
y yo, sigo caminando, buscando la reencarnación

talking

te
lo
digo
bien
claro
tenemos
que
buscar
firmeza
tenemos
que
buscar
firmeza
firmeza
tenemos
que
trabajar
la
vida
pague
o
no
pague
y
después
de
la
firmeza
uno
puede
hasta
vacilar
por
largos
ratos.

praying

papá dios está agallao, ya no puede soportar
los "puerto ricans" están orando overtime
no dejamos dormir a dios, está volviéndose loco
con las comiquerías de nosotros, siempre chavándole
la vida, papá dios está prendío, los "puerto ricans"
están "overloading the circuits with numerous requests"
te lo juro, créemelo, yo te lo advertí, lo escribí,
papá dios está enfogonao, deme esto, consígame
aquello, dele luz a mi vida, la com puta dora
tiene corto circuito, las operadoras "complaining"
a la supervisora, "qué diablo' hablan esas viejas,
rezan el rosario, murmurando como hormigas, their
spanish is unintelligible, they pray too fast"
dios-te-salve-maría-llena-eres-de-padre-nuestro-
gloria-al-padre-y-a-las-galletitas-y-el-chocolate-
caliente-amén, we don't understand.

the angels brought a lawsuit to the supreme
court of heaven, protesting puerto rican prayers
"we cannot pick up their signals, them puerto rican
ladies, they pray non-stop, when they pray, they
pray for everybody, their prayers are over-
flowing their allotted time, and it's working
against you, papá dios, we cannot answer their
prayers, they must be wondering, 'how come papá
dios does not reply?' they are taking over
the english channels, we cannot identify the items,
judge strictly for yourself, look at this daily sample,
just those pentecostals alone are driving the holy
spirit insane, all they want is transformations,
transformations, we're not coming down on them
puerto rican bodies, those crazy people are praying
themselves into our jobs, all they want are crazy
indian angels to come down, to assist some crazy
spiritualist, and we don't understand those native
dialects, papá dios, please change the laws."
papá dios got up and said . . . "Bendito, they work so

hard, bendito, they are so passive, i never get
angry with my worthy faithful subjects, it is
just that some crazy puerto rican poet is misinforming
the people, i'm not enfogonao," papá dios ordered
a new computerized system to solve the inundation
problem, but papá dios said to please tell them
puerto ricans that he'll listen to their every
desire, if they will give papá dios un brakecito,
concho, "y déjenme dormir. De vez en cuando
duerman ustedes, por favor."

dancing

i'll go out dancing
in the heat of salsa
i'll go out dancing
the adventures of my choice
i'll go out dancing
casablanca-corso-ochentas
broadway ninety-six style
i'll go out dancing
silk and gold and high-tech
french ala italiana dressed
in latino modern dress
i'll go out dancing
moving it, feeling it
living it, holding it
live and disco music
i'll go out dancing
hips that swing, curves expanding
dancing, the coro is chanting
dancing, turns entangling
dancing, sonero attacking
dancing, percussion bombarding
dancing, brass reacting
dancing, steps are snapping
música, música, música, música
clave-clave, clap, clap, clap
dancing, dancing, dancing
i'll go out dancing
heads underneath the cymbals
hands gouging pianos
everything touching
dancing, bodies integrating
dancing, climaxing, sweating
dancing, dancing
the night is wild
no sense of time
i'll go out dancing
salsa society dancing

and i danced
dancing
totally
digging
giving
and
we danced
the night
away
we danced
the night
away.

Politics

political

i'm pushed, i'm being pushed, pushed,
i'm pushed, i'm being pushed, pushed,
into the gutter, i'm being pushed,
into boiling point anger,
i'm being pushed, pushed,
yet i retain control,
yet i lean back,
yet i turn the other cheek,
yet i look to god for patience,
i'm being pushed, pushed,
into violent verbal action,
that tells me something,
i must do something i must
contribute to my community,
i must get involved,
i'm pushed, i'm being pushed, pushed,
yet i take alternative roads,
to keep away from the involvement,
because community leadership,
leads to broken marriages,
leads to lack of trust,
you do and do for the people,
and the people will stab you
in the back, so, i do nothing,
but knock on cold steel
with a rubber hammer,
attempting to penetrate,
until my soul no longer sweats,
but then, one day, i heard
music on the other side of
steel and i wrote down the
lyrics, marching with every
beat, shooting bullets of words
i sang the tune with my friends,
malice and injustice pushed again
and i made a citizen's arrest.

commonwealth

no, not yet, no, not yet
i will not proclaim myself,
a total child of any land,
i'm still in the commonwealth
stage of my life, wondering
what to decide, what to conclude,
what to declare myself.

i'm still in the commonwealth
stage of my life, not knowing
which ideology to select.

i'm still in the commonwealth
stage of my life, all of us
caught in a web of suspension,
light years away from the indians'
peaceful enclaves.

i'm still in the commonwealth
stage of my life, observing
the many integrated experiences
we took everything
and became everybody else.

i'm still in the commonwealth
stage of my life, but there's
not enough hatred in our hearts
to kill each other or to draw
blood for too long. ours
is a mental search
carved through a mainstream of options
but yet, somewhere
in the commonwealth, we all yearn
to feel our strengths,
to show our ultimate,
to find common wealth among us,
to close our eyes,

to find the total silence, silencio, silence,
to find . . . not one thing that unites us,
even in silence we are still
in the commonwealth stage of our lives
so let's touch hands, friends and foes,
and stay together to hear each other's
sounds just for one moment, let's stay
tucked together, and maybe then, less
options, maybe then, hope.

dictador

nosotros hemos controlado por muchos
siglos aquí, así que, no queremos
fuerzas militares, a menos
que se evolucionen con nuestros
intereses propios, y por eso, yo le
digo a nuestro pueblo que resista
a los comunistas, hay que apoyarme
a mí, yo negociaré, por mi derecho
propio, y les prometo que haré todo
lo posible, para que en mi presidencia
las únicas armas en este país sean
las que yo les compre a nuestros grandes
amigos democráticos de los estados
unidos, diariamente hablo con los más
altos niveles militares de los americanos, y ellos nos han garantizado la
paz; así que, no tienen nada que du-
dar, trabajen la tierra, no hablen,
ruéguenle mucho a dios, odien a todos
los políticos, no jueguen con armas,
porque el fuego es el padrino de los
cementerios, paguen sus impuestos
religiosamente y esperen que yo ter-
mine los planes preliminares para
desarrollar y después planificar,
y después votar por el plebiscito,
si es que sí o no debemos de votar;
este proceso se coge mucho tiempo
pero yo les juro que el próximo
presidente de esta nación será elec-
to por el pueblo, esperen un anuncio
pronto, sigan su máximo respaldo a
mi gobierno, centralmente adquiriendo
una posición internacional, he terminado
un tour del french riviera y les habla-
ré mañana directamente de italia, se
despide su gran elocuente presidente

de esta gran nación, y ustedes el gran
pueblo de este gran país, en éste su
exclusivo canal satélite de televisión,
y éste su único programa, que dios
siempre bendiga nuestra bandera, todos
a dormir, es hora del curfew, apagaré
toda la electricidad, todos a rezar,
bien calladitos, buenas noches, este
discurso fue pregrabado, gracias.

revolutionary

it
is
no
myth
it
has
to
be
resolved
through
blood
to
eliminate
the
ogre
the
permanent
infection
the
cancer
must
be
killed
it's
historically
clear
to
us
who
wage
constant
war
against
oppression
death

to
   all
      oppressors
       free
        all
           political
             prisoners
               humanity
             and
               world
                 peace
                  stop
                   the
                     bomb
                    love
                      knows
                     no
                        compromise

popular

limbo
limping in circles
still buying time
the indecision of goals
still buying time, the leftists
and the rightists, and the left
right of all parties always
recruiting your unbalanced
members, like the jehovas and the
pentecostals preying on catholic
members, tired of european non-
spanish preachers, but the elders
in the social clubs and
muñoz are still your strongest
allies, and you're saved by
the mathematical dominoes of
so many puerto rican indecisions
and so many speculations, but
your soul moves in listless
circles turning like the old
man carousel, turning like the
old man carousel.

don luis muñoz marín

the poet jorge brandon, a sacred father-testament,
praises your history, your expansion, your moving
us into the center of the modern nineteenth century,
where man is most advanced, as we left the motherland,
the adventure of your policies and, most important,
the elders always speak of Constitution Day, in which
our flag, la bandera, was raised officially for the
first time, that moment, the free associated state,
or in historical terms, the commonwealth, that day,
muñoz, the elders hold in divine respect, there is
patriot in your name, muñoz, they gave you an up-
lifting walk, in the trains of your people's hand,
and they buried you with full honors, muñoz.

now i find traces of your bohemian days in the lower east side,
where you cleansed yourself, where you devised the
visions of your plans, where sometimes you won now
at the expense of future, but they love you, muñoz,
in the social clubs, the dominoes, the "palito," for
that day, it was an honorable and intelligent compromise,
it gave us time, they said you only went half way,
but you did not sell all the way, and the puerto
rican flag was up flying, out of a quietly persistent
struggle throughout its history, somehow your
pragmatic element was a necessary step onward, the
elders taught me to respect you, but you were in the
best of companies, the poet, jorge brandon, is
willing to defend you in front of anybody, and
i tell you, muñoz, that's one man i listen to
right away, and i tell you, thank you, for buying
time, no matter what else is ever said, the elders
believe in you and i believe in the elders.

don luis a. ferré

there were no paintings
and no poems in his name,
the young artists painted albizu,
he started thinking of his grave,
don luis a. ferré fell asleep,
a vision came his way:

instead of state senator of the u.s.a.,
why not governor of an independent state,
of a puerto rican-japanese state,
methodologies and third world training,
protecting the interests of the u.s.a.,
teaching english and spanish,
to african and latin american states,
plenty of money and military bases,
and a faithful ally of the western world.

there were no paintings
and no poems in his name,
the young artists painted albizu,
he started thinking of his grave,
don luis a. ferré fell asleep,
a vision came his way:

why not the patriot ferré?
he could move the new progressive party,
to major cities of the u.s.a.,
and still be elected u.s. senator in florida
and eat crumbs two ways,
in puerto rico and in the u.s.a.

puerto rico, independence, yes,
estadistas still in power, yes,
all his enemies will pay tribute,
at least for that one day,
his memoirs will be published,
he will be quoted on the front page

of the n.y. times,
"it took me, the capitalist ferré,
to complete what the pragmatist muñoz
and the revolutionary albizu
had started long ago."
don luis a. ferré awoke,
he was highly perplexed,
one of his dreams had said, "yes."

socialista

no debe ser así, que ellos son prejuiciados
y excluidos, porque ellos expresan
su santa patriótica libertad, la búsqueda
de un más-abierto humanismo
y no se quejan de ser minoría, y hablan
claro, y son apabullados y acusados y ellos
siempre empujando, la contrariedad a los
beneficios de la ciudadanía se expresan los
teoréticos-pintores, folklore soberanía,
colores de país libre, rojo-poderoso-verde-fuerte
junto también al mar, desarrollándose todo,
el conjunto en las antillas se expresan
los que cantan el nuevo camino,
sus verdades se vuelven dicha en gran futureo
por las carreteras del paso-paso,
por las carreteras del paso-paso,
por las carreteras de dicha-dicha,
lo llevan al tronco, la montaña independencia,
la celebración era bien alta, bien hundida,
subiendo banderas, esperando las estrellas,
al compás sublime de la libertad, así que,
no debe ser así, que ellos sean menospreciados,
porque en cualquier corte, brother, a ellos
se les pueden entregar nuestras tierras, y en
cualquier cuadro se llenaría de las riquezas
más puras, pero al final, lo que
importaba era la tremenda responsabilidad
que llevaba la causa y la tremenda realización
que todavía nada se había perdido, y la tremenda
sensación de elogiar, tantos buenos compatriotas
del pasado, cuyos esfuerzos no fueron en
vano, y lo tremendísimo-más-grande, qué linda
es la bandera de puerto rico, flotando
sus quehaceres celestiales ruiseñoreándose con los
planetas al compás de su himno, declamado
por su pueblo, y su estrella, sola entre las estrellas.

mari bras

la
in
de
pen
den
cia
no
se
com
pra
no
se
com
pro
me
te
se
a
ga
rra
des
de
las
ra
í
ces

licenciado don pedro albizu campos

like the year eighteen ninety-eight
        a definitely pure-white-clear poem.
        "tierra, tierra, desamparada . . ."
like the year nineteen ninety-eight,
        a patriot when he lived,
        a patriot when he died
        became a definitely
        pure-white-clear poem:
            "tierra, tierra, aislada,
            "tierra, tierra, despreciada . . ."
like all the time you talked
to us, principled, as the
desperate one who pulls switch-
blades protecting turf,
        a hero whose grave is san juan's
        capitolio overlooking la perla
        sanctified by a definitely
        pure-white-clear poem.
            "tierra, tierra, eres mía,
            manoseada mía, despreciada
            mía, mía, yo te daré pecho."
you who never smiled,
we see your face, fighting
all attacks, everybody
loves you, condemns you
you conservative radical
of the nineteenth century,
your nationalism drove
deep down into our future,
        a delicate man revered in the streets,
        don pedro is don pedro is don pedro
        pedro and again he will ever live,
        as long as we're alive we praise a
        definitely pure-white-clear poem.
        such is the testament of his:

"borinquen, tierra mía,
divina, celosa, No Estado,
humana nación."
and proud like a definitely
pure-white-clear poem,
don pedro albizu campos,
forever imbedded in our souls.

AmeRícan

we gave birth to a new generation,
AmeRícan, broader than lost gold
never touched, hidden inside the
puerto rican mountains.

we gave birth to a new generation
AmeRícan, it includes everything
imaginable you-name-it-we-got-it
society.

we gave birth to a new generation,
AmeRícan salutes all folklores,
european, indian, black, spanish
and anything else compatible:

AmeRícan,   singing to composer pedro flores' palm
                 trees up high in the universal sky!

AmeRícan,   sweet soft spanish danzas gypsies
                 moving lyrics la española cascabelling
                 presence always singing at our side!

AmeRícan,   beating jíbaro modern troubadours
                 crying guitars romantic continental
                 bolero love songs!

AmeRícan,   across forth and across back
                 back across and forth back
                 forth across and back and forth
                 our trips are walking bridges!

it all dissolved into itself, an attempt
was truly made, the attempt was truly
absorbed, digested, we spit out
the poison, we spit out in malice,
we stand, affirmative in action,
to reproduce a broader answer to the
marginality that gobbled us up abruptly!

AmeRícan,   walking plena-rhythms in new york,
strutting beautifully alert, alive
many turning eyes wondering,
admiring!

AmeRícan,   defining myself my own way any way many
many ways Am e Rícan, with the big R and the
accent on the í!

AmeRícan,   like the soul gliding talk of gospel
boogie music!

AmeRícan,   speaking new words in spanglish tenements,
fast tongue moving street corner "que
corta" talk being invented at the insistence
of a smile!

AmeRícan,   abounding inside so many ethnic english
people, and out of humanity, we blend
and mix all that is good!

AmeRícan,   integrating in new york and defining our
own destino, our own way of life,

AmeRícan,   defining the new america, humane america,
admired america, loved america, harmonious
america, the world in peace, our energies
collectively invested to find other civilizations, to touch God, further and further,
to dwell in the spirit of divinity!

AmeRícan,   yes, for now, for i love this, my second
             land, and i dream to take the accent from
             the altercation, and be proud to call
             myself american, in the u.s. sense of the
             word, AmeRícan, America!

Mixturao and Other Poems

Folklores

Word

(for the bard jorge brandon)

"Poetry was meant to be heard
poetry was meant to be read"
indomitable companions
interactions
simultaneously
quivering reader
fullest sensorial
written realizations

                    "Poetry was meant to be read"
                    silent reading internality
                    between eye-of-I
                    involved in total
                    self-absorption
                    capturing intellect
                    treasures pleasures
                    orgasmic intonations
                    dignified silence
                    intimately touching
                    at innermost

"Poetry was meant to be heard"
spoken word
oral transmission
listener exposed to
vocabularies
ear's timpani
exploration vowels
consonants physically
muscling personal
voices integrated
stimulated tonalities

                    so read deep in
                    so read out loud
                    drench two communions
                    enjoy inventive historical
                    all-time coup d'gras.

nideaquinideallá

de qué i know yo sí sé
backnforth here soy de aquí
regreso dicen y qué what
aterricé o acá o allá

my first name is de aquí
my last name is de allá
my last name is nideaquinideallá
yet-to-be defined
evolucionario hybrid

backnforth here soy de aquí
cannot be defined
cannot be categorized
cannot be pasteurizao
cannot be homogenizao

what's my new name?
¿cómo me dicen?
regreso a mi tierra nativa
me llaman y qué what
les contesto somos
we are the children
immigrant/migrantes
our madres cutting
blood crowns entering
fronteras wired fences
nuestros padres wrinkled
foreheads peso of dollar-
an-hour miseria
our uncles and tías
flesh-skinned manos
see-through cemented
tenements hard-core trabajo
mis hermanos and sisters
open-preyed borders
societal disasters

de qué i know yo sí sé
in my yet-to-be defined
birthplace homeland
dual citizenship accusations
indignations differentiations
pesadillas de callos
intellectual displacements
transplanting raíces
aquí no allá yes aquí allá
backnforth no sé si maybe
in between schizophrenia
cultural ataques in all
directions hip-hopping
nightmares paralyzing
incertidumbres frenéticas

aterricé o acá o allá
child of western hemispheric
creations ancestral inheritors
not knowing past three
previous generations
my boricua sobrenombre
original by parent's birth
caribbean by folklore
hispanic by culture
nuyorican by geographic
migrational displacements
latino by mutual promotion
urban by modern necessity
offspring of indigenous dialectics
too many hats to wear
too little time to square
qué vida what a life

i'm in the usa of america
and in us of a, you suffer
insignias of apathy
prejuicio subtle racism
minority status

us of a, you suffer
watching our nation invading other nations without an invitation

my middle name is de allá
constant anti-nuyorican
anti-latino born wedlock
on u.s. soil bilingual
problemas not me anymore
we in all of us ustedes
siempre malnombrándonos
we fight not to be brainwashed
so se acabó el relajo
stop mental disenfranchisement
my last new latest name:

       nideaquinideallá
       impossible to blend
       impossible to categorize
       impossible to analyze
       impossible to synthesize
       our guerrilla cultural camouflage
       survival linguistic construction
       at emergency moment's notice
       complex afirmaciones parametric
       principles fermenting
       secretive universal
       garabatopandegato
       continental yearnings
       complex jerigonza
       de mi hablar

       nideaquinideallá
       escríbelo junto
       sin letra mayúscula
       gracias

latino

we are from here
bred to win
family's ambitions
aspirations upward
mobility adelante
centers of advancement
alluring mixtures
healthy-looking razas
societal experimenters
multi-rhythmic embracers
musically popping top charts
blending gracefully
limited economic
power operators
struggling at bottom
ladder entry points
concluding that our pride
cannot settle for crumbs
hand-me-downs so
we don't open our eyes
we never close them.

southwest border trucos

when you see mexicanos
progressing in your barrios
working for los coreanos
cooking for all new yorkers
pressing laundry garments
winning international marathons
receiving two dollars an hour
undocumented non-card misery
remember they represent
a free independent nation
thirty million largest latino population
nachos, salsa, burritos, guacamole
mariachi, national folklore taco bell.

when you see mexicanos ilegales
selling fruit and flowers in all kinds of weather
bow your head
to a formidable free nation
to a great latino people
to a great hispano nation
la voz de aztlán speaking indeed!

"estoy celebrando la migra deftness, chuy,
pues ahorita te cuento, cuate,
somos five-hundred-year-old dueños
of united states territories, pinche güey.
we have over fifty percent español
linguistic ownership west of the mississippi, ese.
we owned the west-oeste before thirteen
colonies gringos' imperialist western expansion
militaristically illegally annexed us, carnal.

"pues, ahorita te cuento, compadre.
la cellular walkie-talkie ten-four security
alguaciles boundary between el paso, texas, y
juárez, méxico, los americanos protestan que la
bandera mexicana scaling cincuenta pies de
altura y cincuenta pies de ancha dominates all

billboards leading to el aeropuerto de la
borde entre estados unidos la ten-four nos
vigilan our illegal entry so that we don't
cross into our original fronteras from our
squatter housing.

"qué cabrones ignorantes.
nosotros somos
lifetime experts of río grande historia, vato.
somos administradores of el río certification
notary services international consortium, carnal.

"pues, ahorita te cuento, madre,
las mujeres de la noche conocen the hourly
shift of americanos patroling su enchilada
lunch breaks and the gringos' eight-men rosters, mano.
las mujeres occupy leadership positions in
counter-intelligence. they also monitor their
boozing hábitos en las tavernas, hombre.

"nosotros, daily sponsors of buy-one-get-two
tequilas paid by the council of cruzados,
save ten percent of our underground
collection fees for supporting services of
young mexicano undergraduate students at
ut el paso and new mexico aggies. they
submit to us general profiles of los rednecks
hired to arrest us, padre.

"the civil servants are non-college upper-lower-
class up to their necks with installment payments.
they cash their checks en las tavernas, are uneducated
on budget plans, and are abusive of spouses unattentive to
children's growth. Son simples brutos generally they
only capture us asleep or borrachos, qué chingadera.

"también tenemos computer charts. we know they are
slow por las mañanitas cuando no hay tráfico. uno
cruza feliz the border. supervisor sabe de las
redadas de la ICE buscando las drogas las veinte y
cinco mil maneras creativas to smuggle pero el

teniente ellae likes las prostitutas especially
la madame emma la pollona singing con
mariachis mientras she stripteases. en la
oficina we make xerox copies of their weekly
raids usually occurring after five for overtime
benefits, mi hermano.

"but, what the hell, carajo, we cross el
río grande veinte y cuatro horas a day a comer los
mcdonalds at university pizzerias, macho. we
offer daily tours to potential immigrants. les
llenamos los papeles del social security. we have
cincuenta maneras to penetrate backnforth, primo.

"le metemos sleeping pills en las fajitas de guacamole,
adobamos el lime de las coronas con horny ingredients
picantes para que se les paren los chingues.
rentando cuartos, we press their
uniformes with green pepper ajillos calientes
pa' que se rasquen las nalgas to complain and bitch with the
sun's heat and leave media hora tempranito, carnalito.

"we have bachillerato trasnocheros trucos de
apache y si nos agarran in the u.s. of a. they just
send us across to our frontera suburban squatters.

"but ultimately sabemos que nuevo méxico,
texas, california, arizona y colorado
are always nuestras tierras. we come-enter a
nuestro gusto, con ganas. estas
fronteras son mexicanas, de méxico, compadrito.
ajúa, cholo, chale, ese no la chingues.
canta, gallito cross without concern
nuevo méxico es terreno de pancho villa."

mayanito

way up there on top of clouds
above the rain linkages
western hemispheric mountains
nearing heaven
mayanito looking down
observing rain below
descending upon continental
earth with generous showers . . .

mayanito saddened that
mountain clouds are not
blessing him
prayed to higher sources
old civilizations
centuries of rituals
celestial spirituals . . .

mayanito awakened in
early morning with
mighty gods united
torrential warpath
thundering warriors . . .

mayanito's observed miracles
gigantic raindrops
landing powerfully
one by one
nature's canopy
like tiny soldiers
bouncing briskly
silent bombs plunging . . .

mayanito in fields of eternity
playing marbles rain lluvia
drops dancing-n-marching
joyfully rank-n-file
newlyfound friends
nature's amigos.

sur americano

europeanismos genéricos piel de sociedades
centro generaciones caudillistas /
imperios militares exclusivos golpes de estado
complejos indígena campesinos bajando sus
pandillas reclamando años de opresión
la tierra potente de recursos la droga
exclusiva adictiva el placer mundial controversial
minerales esperando los hierros que penetren
sus entrañas dándole luz a exclusiva clase alta
millonarios base del hemisferio la segunda
europa española con cien dialectos de negros
indígenas en contra punto de 27 dialectos
españoles añádele el portugués los italianos
alemanes integrados inglaterra reclamando
el fútbol deporte importante fuerza
mundialmente conocidos su música corazones
pulpo de expresiones tango bonito boleros cumbias
andinas vallenatos salseros pulmones bellezas
mujeres aclamadas universo literatura al alto
majestuoso se traduce sus lúminas raíces
inmediatamente a dar a luz guerrilleros campesinos
institucionalizando nuevos estados armados
océanos montañas todavía naturales la pobreza
epidémica embajada de militantes revolucionarios
visionarios abogando colores indígenas
con cien dialectos regionales
rodeando la exclusividad sociedades media
alta intelectual avanzada distinguido desarrollo
potencial cuando el dólar se convierta en pan
americano sólo una moneda como europa.

puerto rico's chupacabras

following confirmed researched sightings apparitions
sanctioned hemispheric telescopers consortium
galaxy study approved milky way council of
strange phenomena p.o. box 15 jupiter moon
data cum da cum space planet x int. net web site
chupacalabrium council hijas de maría venus
chapter sighting's daily report.

chupacabras is the following:

> a mezcla-cockfight ducha boricua
> pulsars and quasars meteor showers
> ionosférico platillo volador radio
> signals linked arecibo's sinkhole
> observatory se estalló un cometa
> giving birth to an extra-terrestrial
>
> "déjate de cuentos, brother, yo lo vi
> porque me lo contó mi abuelita que
> masca tabaco y es medio ciega
> sitting in her veranda at twelve o'clock
> ella me bipeó en la celular she told me
> that deep into el yunque rain forest
> an international gathering of coquís
> tired of being heard not seen
> palpitated themselves into a frenzy
> consortium orchestral symphonic
> mellifluous acapellos y nació un fantasma."
>
> "qué sabes tú, mal educao, la chupacabras es
> un acidic petro chemical pharmaceutical
> residue illegally deposited blended arrabal
> with an encountered santería witchcraft
> brujos by-the-sea espiritista demonic séance
> es un trabajo del diablo, sacúdete, satanás."

"compañeros, vamos a llegar al cráneo intelectual
nuestra posición es la siguiente: in this puerto
rican island full of conflicts and political
indecisions the nation floating in listless circles
dando vueltas como el viejo carrusel
tuvimos un sueño colectivo empezamos
a halucinarnos en un estado esquinillazofrénico."

"es que esos socialistas hablan y no se entiende
ni un comino, la pura realidad es que chupacabras
es un movimiento independentista
es un multi-party umbrella strategy
creating new medicinologies to supplant
the island research grants y ahora pagamos
peaje tres cincuenta por minuto en la internet
compañía nacionalista y lolita lebrón
la dueña del chupacabras web site."

"óigame, consorte, ven acá, déjame leerte las
barajas en mesa blanca págame cinco pesos
por la consulta los espíritus me dicen
que la chupa es un agente de la f.b.i.
que las cabras son awacs surveillance
están documentando el nalgueo de los fundillos
de activistas buscando información
de los terroristas, cuídate."

"esa gente está craqueá, que tú crees de eso
yo soy él y ella que camina las noches
en las barrancas buscando ambiente
yo soy director y directora de la farándula
let me tell you the real deal, la chupacabras
surgió de un halloween costume party
lagartijos y lizards sapos transvestial hip-hop
dance psychedelic bisexual underground
rap mezcalinado pitorro moonshine
medical marijuana mixed with ecstasy
píldoras cocainadas mixed with one-hundred-
fifty proof ron don q disguised in one substance.
si con eso no salió la cabra, tú no chupastes."

"brother, lo que tú dijistes es una mentira total
¿vistes?, mi pana, en puerto rico no bebemos
el chupacabras is an organizational secret
boricua password palabra secreta, mano
borinquen hysteria vampiric mascota es un
equipo que juega doble en liga extra-terrestial."

"pueblo, the puerto rican people are always
being duped, compañeros, después de un
análisis intenso hemos concluido que la
entre comillas 'chupacabras' is the, cito,
'commercialization imperialist relajo-joke'
end of cito, cito twice entre comillas 'is the
promotion of un nuevo trago para embabucarnos
mixed with cranberry orange juice
muy delicioso, sabes, served with bacardi
vampire teeth flying en cualquier esquina
sponsored by el lumpen sector camera de
comercios chapter of unemployed teamster
piragüeros,' end of cito, cito twice."

"cállate, zafao, vete a trabajar pa que me mantengas
el gallo cucurucú es el experto de media madrugada
no duermen me contaron que la chupacabras
es la revancha of the puerto rican national pitirre
tired of being depicted as a third-class pájaro
disguising itself."

"la esencia es que un espíritu ambulante
transcendental was touched by the divine
cuatro gold mine of jíbaro sentimientos
y adaptó a la isla, señores, no hay más ná."

"yeah, right, yo soy el incrédulo
there's a chupacabras out there,
and jesus christ ascended into
heaven in a ufo, yeah, right."

"the ultimate reality dicen los chamaquitos
que es un cartoon superhero scaring nightmares
walt disney theme park production for the
caribbean basin."

"aquí lo que hay es un catálogo de tostaos,
yo soy la única religiosa que reza rosario
de la virgen maría en las iglesias pentecostales,
el chupacabras es la atalaya, the armageddon
is coming, el fin del mundo, es un invento
de los testigos de jehová para vender
periódicos en las esquinas."

"and me, too, nuyorican, bro, I'm chupacabras'
illegitimate nephew street-vendor pestering
you to purchase this t-shirt taped account
Kodak moment for $16.95 take five bolita
winning numbers, what a bargain!"

"finalmente llegamos a la conclusión que el
chupacabras es el espíritu de toño bicicleta
protected from the authorities by the puerto
rican nation toño celebrated his every escape
ritualistically drinking virgin goat blood
he killed them with two souvenir plastic
machetes like the spanish toreadores who
beben sangre when they kill the toros
this document is sponsored by peta's
brigitte bear-all as god acknowledged
lo que habíamos percibido
que puerto rico es 100 x 35 x 1000
historias chupacabra folktales
breeding creatively nuestras mitologías."

Fronteras

indigenous

stomp your feet
affirm you live
on stolen lands
native peace pipers
WAKAN God-sun
twenty-eight directions
worshipping earth's
sweat lodge
cleansing bird's
multi-tongue speakers

stomp your feet
to advanced civilizers
pow-wow heart drum
WACIPI feast
real estate owners
multi-trillion illegal
treaties hidden inside
university historical
municipality vaults
constitutionalizers
legal eagle vultures
hemispheric brutal
holocaust

stomp your feet
shout-out in demand
shout-out all at once
"give them their land
or give them reparation"

stomp your feet

español

entonces out of our spiritual resolve
we began to create con tu diploma
apellido de la nada adentro de
rutas migratorias producción
de nuevas culturas
nuestras guaguas recogiendo
las frutas de tar-brea fría
en la migra los callos
are re-cycled en un cuero
duro tremendo bilinguazo
de pobreza nos abandonastes
nos vendistes, you sold us out.

ahora nuestra piel esquinillera
te adoba with palabras migrantes
en el hemisferio cross-roots fertilizing
sueños podridos stitched inside
singer machines.

now, we, gente de sangre gorda
metiéndole miedo a tu real academia
española cucándote con millones de
palabras continentales trabalenguas
enmixturadas cocinándose en asuntos
hemisféricos combinando lingüísticas
en proporciones humanas.

el español sagrado es una frontera jíbara
indígena con modismos dichos negristas
criollismos mitologías de melaza manteca
españolizada interlingüe con betún.

now the world anxiously awaits our noveleros
cuentistas poeteros modernistas armados con
lenguas multi-mixtas con crónicas documentando
we existed before we discovered colón.

el español sagrado sucursal de invasión de árabes y gitanos
experimentos enmixturados like the twenty-
seven dialectos you speak España conquistadora
you took the gold leaving us powerless
forcing our imperialistic caudillo struggles
to reconstruct your traditional European lengua
creating our western hemispheric tongue.

but alas i love you Spanish
half of my lengua
part of my tongue
i'm gonna fight for you siempre i am
your humble son
qué tragedia
qué contra
dic ci ón.

tesis de negreza
(*canción de bobby capó*)
(*reseña del dr. víctor manuel vega*)

"mataron al negro bembón" → de la canción
negrito cocolo llamado prieto
alborazado blah blah blah

    "mataron al negro bembón"
    ambujo separación
    indistinguida blah blah blah

        "hoy se llora noche y día"
        nos dicen que somos
        calpa mulato iguales blah blah blah

           "porque al negrito bembón"
           cambujos somos unidos
           en este hemisferio chino
           no existe el racismo blah blah blah

              "todo el mundo lo quería"
              coartado burla insensitiva blah blah blah

                "porque al negrito bembón"
                chumbo pueblo antipatía blah blah blah

                  "todo el mundo lo quería"
                  churusco entonces pues:

"y llegó la policía"
cimarrón defensa raza alta bravía

    "y arrestaron al matón"
    sus labios *criollos* suculentos

        "y uno de los policías"
        moreno saboreando sus pupilas

"que también era bembón"
cocolo no la tengo escondida

"le tocó la mala suerte"
cuarterón está aquí mismita

"de hacer la investigación"
soy emancipado para que enrojezcas
con mis cachondos coloreados

"le tocó la mala suerte"
falucho sangre roja mezclada

"de hacer la investigación"
jíbaro de congoleses chupetes
labios de erección grandiosa

"y sabe la pregunta"
grifo montañas sutil dulzura

"que le hizo al matón"
ladino betunando emoción
borinqueñosos poros

"porque lo mató"
liberto temblor besos volcánicos
del cielo viniste y devolviste

"diga usted la razón"
manumiso internas calenturas

"y sabe la respuesta"
mestizo profundas entrañas

"que le dio el matón"
moreno rosando sus raíces:

"yo lo maté por ser tan BEMBÓN"
morisco le contesta
voy a sacar la lengua para limpiarte
de tus sutiles prejuicios

 "el guardia escondió la lengua y le dijo"
 soy *niche* para insultarte cuando me insultes
 para confrontarte cuando tu ignorancia
 desigualdad escupe estereotipos
 soy *lobo* voy a sacar la bemba patriótica
 colectiva humana cuando me respetes
 amistosamente

  "ésa no es razón"
  soy *loro* voy a sacar la bemba
  la que nunca había escondido

"para matar al bembón"
soy *mulecón* bemba enmelezada
con cien millones de negros
continentales

 "ésa no es razón"
 soy *muleque* marca de hierro
 caliente lacerado marca de *carimbo*

  "huye huye"
  soy *moyeto* aquí la segunda áfrica
  dividida por yemayá

   "que ahí viene el matón"
   soy *negro pardo* que se
   aparezca el matón

    "ésa no es razón"
    soy *quinterón* lo confronto
    con bembazo indigno

"yo te digo que viene"
soy *retinto* valiente ciudadano

"cortando bembas"
soy *saltoatrás* arresto
al criminal canalla

"ya se la cortó"
soy *tente en el aire*
    investigo la letra de bobby capó
"al negrito bembón"
      soy *torno atrás*
        analizo la grabación
          de rafael cortijo
            los soneos dulce creativos
            de ismael rivera
              soy *zambaigo*
                critico mi-tato-pecado
                  repito mil veces este folklore
                "ésa no es razón"
                  soy *zambo* bemba escopeta
                  sacude bemba gloriosa
                    "esconde la bemba" nunca
                    mas soy un majestuoso
                    BEMBÓN.

spanglish

pues estoy creando spanglish
bi-cultural systems
scientific lexicographical
inter-textual integrations
two expressions
existentially wired
two dominant languages
continentally abrazándose
en colloquial combate
en las aceras del soil
imperio spanglish emerges
control pandillaje
sobre territorio bi-lingual
las novelas mexicanas
mixing with radiorocknroll
condimented cocina lore
immigrant/migrant
nasal mispronouncements
baraja chismeteos social club
hip-hop prieto street salsa
corner soul enmixturando
spanish pop farándula
standard english classroom
with computer technicalities
spanglish is literally perfect
spanglish is ethnically snobbish
spanglish is cara-holy inteligencia
which u.s. slang do you speak?

encimitadelinglés

encimitadelinglés, nené
apabullando sus tonalities
con el keeping-up
five hundred palabras
they invent every week

encimitadelinglés, nené
intimately touching
caressing her limb's existence
playing with her letras
manipulándola out of
her english-only
ignorancia

encimitadelinglés, nené

la
   com
       puta
          dora
               tenfingering me e-mailing me
            under around underneath
               her teclas
                        wet
                   me
                    mojo

                     into her micro-chips
               into her macro-soft tela
               into her hard wares
               telecom-municating me
               electrically wiring me
               wet-me-mojo enfermito
               soy cortejo of her
               majestic spider
               web-page-ness
estoy encimitadelinglés, nené

bilingüe

exploring and dissecting
texto bilingüe
definiendo canción
nacional sylvia rexach
olas y arenas with
standard poetic spanglish

soy la arena   finely grained crystals
que en la playa está tendida   sea-polished
envidiando otras arenas   weightless granules
que le quedan cerca al mar   in a sensual cocktail planted
eres tú la inmensa ola   smoothly naked grounds
que al venir   cha-cha-turned sharp curves
casi me tocas   palm tree english figurines
pero siempre   inviting her olas y arenas
te devuelves hacia atrás   pasando my boricua hands
las veces que te derrama   riding breezes
sobre arenas humedecidas   por tu open bosom
ya creyendo   tidal waves mistress
que esta vez   tu luna yearnings
me tocarás   arriving madrugada's solenmnity
al llegarme   pregnant many periods
tan cerquita   virgin fragility
pero luego te recoges
y te pierdes   into my canela-brown sugar-
en la inmensidad   coated bomboncitos
del mar   melting deliciously . . .

soy la arena   allá in your open pores
que en la playa está tendida   i receive your luscious lips
vive sola su penar   buscándote borinquen
eres ola   your cinammon-powdered
que te envuelves   tongue en mi tierra
en la espuma   somos siete millones
y te disuelves   en múltiples
en la bruma   fronteras lingüísticas

a l e j á n d o t e m e m á s   ya no nos cabe un sola lengua

mixturao
(*for english only*)

we-who engage in
western hemispheric
continental spanish majority
communally sharing linguistics
in humanistic proportions

we-who integrate
urban america
simmering each other's slangs
indigenous nativizing
our tongues' cruising accents
who are you, english,
telling me, "speak only english
or die."

we-who grassroots
and jíbaro dialectics
yodeling mexican riddles
chicano "ese" talk
creole caribbeanisms
black negroid textings
african twisting
european colonizers'
oppressive repertoires
savoring new vocabularies
who are you, English,
telling me, "speak only english
or die."

we-who create continental music
elaborate universal jazz
rhythmic tonalities
vallenato oilings
gospel-rap soulings
brazilian portuguesa
bonito bolero
mayan songs soothing

quebecois hard rock
patois saging
andino cumbias
world-wide tango curvings
merengue-calypso
mating-mixing dancing
tres por cuatro cubanities
con los pasos firmes de aztecas
who are you, english,
telling me, "speak only english
or die."

we-who are at peace in continental
inter-mixtures
do hereby challenge
united states isolationism
anti-immigrant mono-lingual
constitutional bullets
declarations telling us to
"speak only english or die"
"love it or leave it"
spelling big stick carcass
translations universally excluded
multi-lingual multi-cultural
expressions "need not to apply"
who are you, english,
telling me, "speak only english
or die."

so enter our multi-lingual
frontiers become a sharing
partner maybe then I might
allow you the privilege
to call me a tremendous
continental "MIXTURAO."

Mujeres

riqueña hip-hop

yo
me
llamo
borincana
jíbara
puertorra
hermana
me
hinco
toda
en
mi
patria
su
estrella
alta
y
brava
anhelamos
ese
día
en
que
en
plena
carretera
bofeteamos
descarada
cantante
la madona
por arrastrar
sus nalgas
con nuestra
querida
bandera

enrojo
(casi todos y todas . . . miramos . . . pensamos)

she walks . . .

pure
air
divinity
east
harlem
barrio corridors
old-fashioned
cartera
held-in
precious curvings
detalles her
espíritus
protectivos
jealously
guarding
"concho brother"
can't even
touch with words
she walks . . .
so I watched
disimulando from afar
curándome con luscious
adventurous
ashamed-of-myself
enfermito
picantes
calenturas
que me vengo
talking
thinking
por favor
cógeme "pena, nena"
hablando

on behalf of all
my continental
amigos in silence
tirando piropos
atoloquedá

instrument

ivory heads patiently awaiting
countless encounters
daily tightening seductions
fragilities skin-tight lean
nude elegance
all ten fingers feeling up-n-down
they use her moon nocturnal cave
resonating her high peaks
mountain's serenity
resonating
her all-world pitches
they seduce her
she takes all
she wants more she inspires
she stands
deep cuts womb rituals
erection's ecstasy
they proclaim her "la reina de mil nombres"
they acclaim her "the queen of a thousand names"
they undress her ivory petals
they loosen her thin-veiled
see-through nightgown
they encase her velvet smooth blanket
they crown her "tierra"
they call her land "land"
ultimate adulation
"diosa gitana"
    "gypsy goddess"
        "la guitarra"
            they call her
                "the guitar"

milenio

confetti of lágrimas
fantasy tears
landing in san juan manhattan
perfection placed
elegantly sculptured
puerto rican ambiguities
infinite space tears
gotas tearing like
warm church bells-campanitas
new year millennium
past, present, future
lágrimas all in one
effervescent moment
año viejo aguinaldos
despedida tears
choral singing
lustfully auld lang syne
año nuevo
nueva vida
twelve o'clock
las doce celebration
bohemian champagne
poetic brindis
future altar
la danza boricua
dancing libertad
still an añoranza
restless and powerless
cadre confetti of lágrimas
warm gotas raining
like composer rafael hernández
snow flakes melodic tribute
"tilín tilín tilán" landing
softly this new millennium
entering my yet-to-be resolved
political status

tumbadora
(*canto*)

faithful roots tu noble base	tu cum
quinto tiempo landing clave	tu cum cum cum
repicando snapping fingers	tu cum cum cum
armonioso sonero cantar	tu cum
historias tu diosa alabar	tu cum
aquí es que sale el coro	tu cum
prenda preñada	tu cum
cuidando tus loros	tu cum
folclores tesoros	tu cum
caja fuerte que preserva	tu cum
valores africanos	tu cum
sacudiéndote te relajas	**tu cum pru cu tum tum tum**
piel madre la base mulata	**tu cum pru cu tum tum tum**
cuba respire tus pupilas	**tu cum pru cu tum tum tum**
caribe urbaneada	cum
espiritista madama	cum
potencia boricua	cum
nos lleva la clave	cum
reina de las llaves	cum
despojamos	cum
oye bailamos	cum
el coro y el pueblo	cum
gloriosas caderas	cum
long live	**pru cu tum tum tum**
long live	**pru cu tum tum tum**
long live	**pru cu tum tum tum**
	tum tum
	tum tum
	tum tum
	hail our majesty
	touch tumbadora
	our QUEEN!

Hombres

spanglish carta
(*to josé luis gonzález*)

in the fondo of a new york city blackout
i read your stories time
and
time again dos negritos cucándome
mi búsqueda allá adentro
en el bajo hundido manhattan
papote sat on the stoop
en el bajo hundido fanguito
melodía gateaba su famoso baquiné.

arrabal impressions urban
barrio che che colé puente-bridge
crossing from 106th street
boulevard a cuadras de la universidad
de puerto rico todos miramos into el
botecito martín peña filthy infested
alleluia waters spermed putrid residues
comiéndose y tragándose sunday
garbage impuridades absorbiéndose
totalmente condená a muerte
buscando an illusion como cristo
reflections three days old
una melodía se asoma en el fondo
el estomaguito soon to be filled with
aperitivos of waste.

el negrito se asoma
al caño órgano de sonidos
se entrega looking for dance
plena boat en el miedo del caño
at the center an addiction
in martín peña death cursing
from his grave "quién diablos
dio mi nombre a esta gran miseria"
no salty piñones alcapurrias
no luquillo beach jueyes
no el yunque service road pasteles

melodía papote eating nada
comiendo impurities velloneras
screams firecrackers cuerpecito
swimming drowning debajo la
tierra fanguito de borinquen
what a lovely national treasure
infected with negreza ambulante
la miseria ate him up
la patria no lo rescató no se asustó
de este descaro of all ages
ni agueybaná ni los españoles
ni los espíritus prietos se compadrinaron
papote sat on the stoop
melodía solamente lives
inside puerto rican folklore
borinquen se esconde
mientras que el negrito gulp gulp
tragaderos for patches in the asses
melodía gulp gulp gulps estereotipos
patria somos culpables
melodía soy negrito tres veces
vaccinated in lengua prieta
negroide mulatto of no stars
spanglish ebonic disparatero
physical expressions linguistically
crippled with no skies ahorcado
en el fondo fundillo del hoyo fango
clay urinadero no room to breathe
fósiles arqueológicos
sancocho cacadero
eating sopa de microbios
papote sat on the stoop
negrito melodía cocolo prieto
molleto desaparecido infierno
trabalengüero misinformed
blown-up hijo of advanced insularism
melodía papotes descalzos on stoops
of an abandoned nationhood

josé luis gonzález hundió a melodía
en su fondo me fui a buscarlo
read him twenty times upon
the first encounter
me compadrinastes
my creative fuentes born
y poetic dialogue accelerated
como novio en el altar i awaited
your latest pronouncements
to masticate into your phrasings
even then siempre nos cucabas
criticisms of my non-linguistic nada
non-validating me
are you a crucible?
how many reseñas discursos
classroom discussions phd positional
papers inspiring careers with your
marxist pronouncements
from mexican exilio philosophically
advanced universal polemics
national implants
managerial utopias
país de cuatro pisos excluding
papote-melodías
fraternities of humanity.

but you inspired us into
penhood introspection
and we bestow upon you
an african chegüigó
don josé luis gonzález
reminding you that
en el fondo del nuyorican
definitivamente
hay un puertorriqueño.
gracias.

patriota
(to clemente soto vélez)

when i think of clemente soto vélez
i think of an ecumenical document
patriotic humanity

when I think of clemente soto vélez
i think of a social treatise
specialized dignity
ambassadorial leadership
ultimate beso compañero

when i think of clemente soto vélez
i think of camaraderic affection
of his companion AMANDA
clemente's center of all

when I think of soto
illuminating wordsmith
carefully crafting
every letter
chiseling harmonious sounds
molding syllables
shaping words
creating images
bursting streaming
consciousness
directing us into
introspection

when I think of vélez
i think of total independencia
incarcerated militant
la princesa prison
la masacre de ponce

lifetime faithful patriota
passionate speaker
"Qué Viva Puerto Rico Libre"
de cualquier manera in any form
"patria o muerte se lo juro, venceremos."

militant

brothers and sisters, do you want to witness
a virus that is not found in the computer
just take a look at the lifetime breeding
hoodlums daily initiating a mental rape
selling perdition protection ruthless
cowards they are after our community's
health waiting for our children in the
stairs of your streets selling them protection
from sidewalk destiny they use your
weakneses forcing young souls into
drugs criminality offering death scholarships
they infuse inject you with high-powered
certificates methadoning children of early
childhood they create a climate diversion
of fear holding young people hostage
with sedatives enlarging teenage minds
recruiters company prizes best salesperson
of empty dreams lost lives they collect
weekly bonuses for most deformities
in the eyes of our avenues daily we witness
them preying the housing complexes
stationed outside emergency rooms, walk-in
clinics, drugstores, pharmacies offering
painkillers binoculars looking for children
in the school playground community
bodega outpost for those who lack lunches
outside sneakers blockbuster stores wishes
with 3 dollars rent a movie one day free
beeper use instamatic cellulars hip-hop
jeans styled consumerism pressures
they provide the goods for teenagers to achieve
material dreams big-timing our children's
illusions while our social club sellers of
sunday liquor and church service all of us
the rest guilty we watch them washing our

hands like pontius pilate the devil satanic
bandits we blame society social criminal
penal systems our inabilities to confront
the vultures destroying our future.

consignas in brutality
(*shout outs for anthony báez*)

"once again discrimination
blatantly upon our nation . . . "

       no justice, no peace, el silencio nos mata aquí

they shoot us, they club us,
they kill us, they choke us,
open prey to murder, coro

       no justice, no peace, el silencio nos mata aquí

let's protect our community borders

       no justice, no peace, el silencio nos mata aquí

they give justice to police aggressors
courts and judges give them protection

       no justice, no peace, el silencio nos mata aquí

show our rage, show our face
demand justicia all the way

       no justice, no peace, el silencio nos mata aquí

hear the cry, hear the cry,
unfair verdicts, unfair trials
credible witnesses need not apply

       no justice, no peace, el silencio nos mata aquí

let's shout out, let's shout out

       "now everyone together"
       "let's sing and march together"
       "this is a defining moment"
       "total victory we mutter"

"let's demand our civil rights"
"children/people must not die"

no justice, no peace, el silencio nos mata aquí

Trueno . . . Relámpago . . . Lluvia . . . Nieve . . .
Aquí . . . Estamos . . . Unidos . . . Soldados . . .
En Lucha . . . Presente . . .

no justice, no peace, el silencio nos mata aquí
no justice, no peace, el silencio nos mata aquí

preludio barroquero
(*para luis lópez adorno*)

crítica de un concierto para desobedientes
doce años in fermenting adagios
sutiles de la patria allegro palabras
andantes parábolas criollos morales
principled religious mythologies
puerto rican parodies eclectic
inquietudes de carretera voluptuoso
caribe's studious inclusions of
quevedo sílabas imagist ezra pound
mirones jack agüero sonnetic
exactness letras al gorete
palesianismos con ánimo español
24 cenizas ana lydia vega zealotry
guardianship beloved spanish
language expanded a un espíritu
scherzo excomulgado rompiendo
el puro aire clásico palabras
puntiagudas ángel luis méndez
anclas con la muerte en el insomnio
irregular-shaped perlas del caribe
anti-social opposition ambiguous
imageries powerful tensions
flotando en el sub-current aguada
grotesca de cerro gordo this
anti-desconcierto island adorno
rapture-ruptured symphony
obedient dientes de
aliteraciones verbos musculares
ultimate contradictions enchantments
how can you stage a concert
para desobedientes expect anarchy
tumultuousness verbal abuse
expect schizophrenia
expect tomatoes political insurrection

expect social insubordination
adorno destroys and constructs
desobediencia la pava's ultimate
orchestral concierto based in nada?

carpetas in your dossier
(*para ramón bosque pérez*)

walking slowly like the jehovah witnesses
armed with intelligence instruction
they quietly dispersed into all avenidas
boulevards streets and callejones basements
to collect information cia fbi speculators
builders disguised next to you this noche
of every day helicopters high tech chips
in your dossier salieron como hormigas
of all ethnic varieties and moved into el pueblo
gentrification taking place protect your rentas
blowing up cerquillos los building cranes
skyscrapers on 96, 97, 98 streets food emporiums
on 110th street salieron at 2 o'clock
in the morning out of a secret community
meeting place smelling your underwear
investigating vieques peaceful patriotas
mexicanos ilegales arabic suspects
so open your ojos into a citizen's arrest
los trucos agresivos of intelligence
nos-vigilan-ten-cuidao
they transform como las sombras
tienen "control" of two thousand
venas through your pores
nos inyectan por los radio waves
limpiando los cocos con seductive
material conocen that-they-know
el paradero de tus besos secretos
and intimate ten-cuidao
ellos instalan the cable system
al oído de tus nalgas te-lo-juro
that we live en un estado
inconsciente de temor
los awac surveillance supervise y analizan
los granos de arroz that you eat
nos tienen fichao they know
nos tienen embabucao saben

tus mínimos fallos encelulao
tienen cien maneras
to kill you frame you and matarte
they have thousands of agents informers
your most intimate amigo detailing
all your detalles stored in microchips
american scrambled jerigonza
radio microwaved signals
nos tienen limping in circles
desbalanceados with uncertainties
targeted en las entrañas del net-web
lavado de cerebro impeding
your conciencia con un candao of steel
armed with invisible keys
targeting our cultural centers
into ritzy private ownership
tattooing into our schizophrenia
abre los ojos no cojas miedo
ármate with all your resources
ten cuidao

Vecindario

callejerismos

ÓYEME lenguas comunitarias no me eches
la culpa yo soy una simple recogedora bochinchosa
comentando libremente todo lo que tú sabes
no te atreves a decir públicamente pero lo
hablas privadamente así que tranquilo
no saques cuchillas ni me des mal de ojo
no me culpes ni me lleves a la corte
no me acuses de estereotiparlos
como insensitiva pero la lengua que
no es mía comentando que los cubanos
y sus amigos puristas como jerry gonzales
el trompetista siempre con la misma vaina
y que cuba es el centro de la salsa pero
los puertorriqueños son los mejores
arreglistas han mantenido la salsa por
muchos años también son la universidad
de soneros salvaron la salsa como frankie ruiz
suave nueva música raíces farándula amor
con percusión ÓYEME rubén blades
trató y que un crossover con lírica de nueva
canción para ser actor y abogado para perder
las elecciones de panamá pero concho todavía
es el compositor número pedro navaja nos
hace falta su combinación con willie colón
todos sabemos que el merengue es el baile
preferido en los salones de baile en puerto rico
existe un catálogo de bochinches se coge
la noche entera el canario dando
complaint que la puertorriqueña olga tañón
se gana los emmy dominicanos muchos no
saben que los mambo aces roberto roena
fueron los primeros en hacer coreografía con
los coristas no se apuren que yo soy equal
opportunity comentadora de las novelas
mexicanas lloronas con actores de quinta clase
todos tienen guilles de cantante de sexta categoría

pero la thalía la que se casó con mottola
el jefe de sony records la que se quitó dos
costillas y tiró bomba por visitar a la diva
maría félix en el cementerio sin conocerla
está en nueva york para competir
con la diva absoluta number one j lo
personalmente los boricuas acusan a celia cruz
por no apoyar a andy montañez porque los
cubanos de miami no lo dejaron cantar
porque él visitó a pablo milanés en cuba por
eso es que gloria estefan no canta en puerto rico
todos sabemos que la mejor salsa del mundo
se baila por los puerto ricans en orchard beach
pero el merengue es el baile
número uno de latinoamérica simplemente
porque uno nace bailando merengue no hay
que quitar los pies de la pista ÓYEME pero
la balada pop esa y los nuyorican raps se ganan
los emmy platinum como ricky nenudo partido yo
no entiendo cómo santana se hace millonario
con la canción de tito puente "oye cómo va" cuando
los mexicanos ni los chicanos no saben bailar
cha-cha-chá pero selena la del tex-mex era la
más chula del mundo ésa tenía capacidad de
competir con la j lo los nuyorican bailan
como los prietos los chicanos son indios pero
no bailan los dominicanos bailan
salsa a lo izquierdo no vamos a washington
heights a bailar merengue toda la boring noche
pero los boricuas no tienen ni un hit de bomba y
plena en la radio pero su gran folklore
sigue sobreviviendo en las paradas, la calle, el colegio y el hogar
la bachata compite con la salsa y el tex-mex
juan luis guerra el rey de los estudiantes universitarios
hasta el presidente del colegio salió bailando
el dichoso merengue ÓYEME callejerismos así
por el estilo perdónenme pero como no tengo
show de radio ni televisión tengo que hablar ligero

y atoloquedá sintonícense mañana en cualquier
esquina para el próximo comentario de la gran
no-tengo-la-lengua-escondida la fabulosa ÓYEME,
por favor cómprenme este tape por veinte pesos.

el difunto

oye-yeow I'm not entering my compadre's
funeral ni con dos escopetas
amarradas inside my pantaletas

padre

de mis bolsillos not even with
siete velas potencias con cuatro brujos

nuestro que

en mis esquinas haciendo hechizos
oye-yeow I'm not going inside to see

estás

el difunto

en

yeah, from outside in this corner
look at ms. exquisita like she calls
herself the loving daughter

los

la prima de la madrastra
guillándose de ser hija postiza

cielos

she comes for the first time in two años
she lives around the corner

santificado

si a llorar semejantes embustes

sea

she comes a buscar las maletas
que el difunto guardaba

tu nombre

she rented that black dress
from the salvation army

vénganos

she painted false lágrimas
como en las novelas

tu reino

la diablita arrived wearing
un traje red escotao

hágase

she was dancing metal rock
en cbgb all night long

tu voluntad

y qué sorpresa she claims to be
la única hija legítima

aquí

del difunto

en la tierra

she was not a bastard
she claimed the maletas

como en el

belonged to her the rightful heir

cielo

y las dos se agarraron
tooth and nail at the front
door of the funeral parlor
all these cuernos accusations

el pan nuestro

the immigrant priest attempted
to separate them but his
spanish was unintelligible his
english was non-existent
he sounded like a pre-recorded
message while demanding
extreme unction advanced payments

de cada día

el hermano eusebio ex-ministro
of five-dollar mail-order reverendo
licencia re-married with la botella

dánoslo hoy

he was praying with a manguera
of bacardi emerging from
el baúl de su carro

y perdona

oye-yeow te lo digo que manny
el prestamista que dio el
down payment

nuestras deudas

until the social security
releases veteran's insurance
that will arrive in five years

así como

manny quiere cobrarle personalmente
a la viuda desamparada que está
completa

nosotros perdonamos

la viuda with a daughter
another born out of
cuernos y los veinte gatos
so-called socios of gambling
pesetas who brought
the pawn shop guy
to seize up el difunto's
gold-filled tooth-melted
payment of his debts

a nuestros deudores

oye-yeow not me yo no
entro allá adentro ni con
secret service bodyguards

no nos dejes caer

the only decent group
son las viejitas rosary specialists
but they do ten daily visits
pray too fast and cannot be heard

en la tentación

oye-yeow that's why I stay
aquí outside afuera directing
el difunto's last will testament

mas líbranos

please close the coffin and the
ataúd as soon as the doors are
opened no quiero ver ninguna
de estas chaviendas

del mal

that's why I stay outside
en el passing time de pasando
tiempo, oye-yeow, compadre,
descansa en paz

amén

social talk

panamericanismo
con qué se come eso
pues es un pana amigo de américa
es un pan de revoltillo ham & eggs
no lo toques brother, eso es
comunismo castrista in disguise
te van a velar
panamericanism
son los knights of columbus italiano
offshoot national holiday para
amerigo vespucci
algo que tiene que ver con los
prietos de áfrica en el caribe
es un bakery americano en el
east village
un movimiento de universidades
for the lecture circuit
pan es bread de américa pero qué
diablo es un nism ten cuidao eso
tiene raíz de socialism te van a velar
es el nuevo airline de pan am
un movimiento de lingüistas aburridos
las naciones unidas food stamps
o algo por el estilo
una escuela de parachutes
una boring palabra
no es un hit.

harlem elder odes

they walk never afraid of shadows
they emerge unscathed
they turn corners
verbal disputes toned down
criminals pay respect
cooling violent differences
they emerge unscathed
those who dare to hurt them
some say will become
undocumented statistics
inside coffin city morgue . . .

how tenderly sweet antique walk
precious history broad exuberant
smile children's kisses jumping
tenderly into grandpa's loving arms . . .

from far away we prepare to greet
them in awe of dignified charisma . . .

clappings elevated alleluia praying
breaking speed of sound gutting
heaven's soul god's lord spirit

choral harmony finger snapping
hands celestially fathering black love . . .

gospels entrenched down there
clamoring rooted in slavery
digging way down Lord Jesus
high-pitched spirituals sermonized
drum songs polished souls . . .

they pray devoutly thanking God
protecting Harlem from physical danger
transcending church walking home

they spread God's blessings
silent reverence anointed ambassadors
peace for all . . .

soul-good cooking fermented elder's hands
old-fashioned recipes mathematically
proportioned orally passed down
devoured sugar yam pies crusting
ivory teeth conservative baptist
elements "oooming" culinary reviews
meticulous table manners surrendering
temporary licking license marvelously
embellished supported by Jesus
granting sermon's delay to give
almighty god enough time to
resurrect eating out of his second
soul food plate . . .

we talk our outrage
they quietly listen
we criticize
they remain expressionless
we accuse
they say nothing
they guru-listen
so let's repeat what has been
said many times
one never knows what we have
until we lose them
don't take them for granted
cherish them respect them
honor the elder who taught you . . .

innocence
(*to 9/11*)

The day the U.S. lost its innocence,
was a cruel September 11, 2001
historical massacre.

The World Trade Center,
marketed as one acre per floor,
had no central steel beams
supporting its 220 stories.

A devastating mega-bomb,
filled with 157 human atoms,
aboard 2 domestic planes penetrated
the Twin Towers' ready coffins.

A devil cauldron, plotted
with synchronized exactness,
a maliciously curved winged
poisonous dart, aerial death ballet,
plunged the United States under fire,
wounds of war, life in living horror,
paralyzing the world and national psyche.

New York City is in a state of raw war.
Manhattan Island, a battleground zero,
confetti of tears, cemetery of candles,
poster tributes, wall-of-respect collages,
beloved photographs, community hand-
printing urgent requests, carved in paper
stones, outpouring of naked sadness,
looking for miracles, rescue turned to
recovery and removal, ash-laden carnage,
evaporated humans, particle remnants
of 1,000,000 body parts.

Metropolis broken hearts, scars of destruction,
cadre of humanity, healing laments,
consoling souls, army of volunteers,

red cross, blood, food, water, supplies,
counseling armed with prayer-peace,
God's potent weapon, we became
a collective consciousness of one.

Kudos to reflective patriotic and religious music,
parade of family and friends,
triumphant mayor, firefighters,
New York's finest, rescue workers
awarded golden heavenly medals.
A new era of working-
class simple patriots were
supplanting Hollywood's caricatures.
New York skyline a postcard odorous
Wall Street stench death-smoke
companion to Lady Liberty.

We will hold ourselves accountable
for maximum monetary payments
to afflicted families of this national
holocaust.

Perpetrators murdered over
3,000 civilians point blank!
This conspiracy, many years
in the making, map surveillance,
central planning, training, execution,
went unprotected by millions of
defense taxes that we pay.
Massive failure of intelligence services.
Our technology was blinded.
National security devoid of human
informant elements.

Vigorously we now investigate
the military architects of this brilliant insanity,
beyond the usual suspects,
who targeted 4 rockets into the
nerve of our political, military,
economic and civic establishments.

Innocence nevermore!
Our homeland liberty's enchantment
was peace in pieces
molesting ultimate freedoms.
The maiden was exterminated
by virile rugged villians
who loosened America the beautiful
for spacious skies celibate girdles,
who blindfolded her amber waves
of grain immaculate chastity.

Innocence nevermore!
America, home of the brave,
her unblemished naiveté
strapped and strangled,
her national couch
of security abandoned.
All-American wrestlers,
super bad athlete dudes,
hot-shot rally around "U.S.A. U.S.A."
were not alerted by the
organizations that protect us.
They could not protect the Madonna.
Our nuclear AWAC surveillance
pinned by 19 men of doom
sultans' box-cutter blades,
slingshot Davidians leveling
Goliath superpower supremacy
into countrywide submission.
The national flag shredded
in convulsions trembled fears.

Now the nation must flex its muscles,
endowed with world and papal approval
to punish the masterminds,
surrender them to justice,
dead or alive, patriotic cries,
military vengeance!

We are attacked as opulent abrasive infidels.
We are denounced as enemies of
World Order.
We are accused of fracturing ethical
traditional behavior.
We are exporting erotic sexual shamelessness in
the veils of traditional
world beliefs.
We are partisan to Israel.
We must abandon the Persian Gulf.

But we democratically reform our ways
in civilized governance.
We also respond to self-humanity, caring,
sharing, protecting, advising the world.
We have a million counter answers to
your accusations.
We discuss them in civilization.
We don't subject human society as
participants in your sacrifices.

Holy war now jihad emerging once again.
West against no-name nation.
U.S.A. at war with
invisible formidable untraditional
warfare units, highly disciplined,
military-educated logisticians,
cellular networks, anonymous donors,
armed with a martyrdom cell,
unrepentant in ending innocent lives.

Now we close ranks to our borders,
expired visas, deportations our resolve.
Liberty's shores closed the day
our civilians were bombed.
Terrorists implanted psychological
military presence,

acupunctured nerves of patriotism,
aroused suspicion, prejudice,
profiling mistrust.

Living cells in your middle-class
community waiting to unleash
anthrax explosive havoc and mistrust.
We are common suspects
of our daily outings,
strip-searched, detained
rampant fear haunting our
central nervous systems.

We will investigate e-mail
transactions of speculators
cowards who bought insurance
kissed our cheeks and
slashed our throats.

We must not become
vigilantes and discriminators.
Koran Muslim religion is
embellished in love and peace.
Allah, all-knowing, all-powerful,
all-merciful, all-faithful
categorically rejected
terrorists' final prayers.
Mohammed, the great prophet,
never will condone such
blatant and destructive
irresponsibility.

The nation demands:
leadership of unquestionable stature,
leadership versed in the etiquette
of world linguistics,
ambassadorial negotiators,
multi-strategists,
leadership that steers us

into just and peaceful
resolutions to this
long-term conflict
we confront.

We must negotiate with world maturity.
Let's stop this hemorrhage
that achieved its highest expectations!
If you don't close quarters for terrorists,
we will democratically or militaristically
support your opposition.
Counseled to be patient we are impatient.
tooth for tooth, person for person,
city for city, country for country,
we are on alert to destroy you!

The world is responsible to
address this human cry.
The world must protect itself.
Relentlessly we negotiate
anti-war resolutions from
committed nations.
Time is short. 62 countries
lost citizens in the rampage.

Yet our nation must transcend
conventional expectations.
But we demand justice!
Explain your irrational destruction
before the eyes of humanity!
Terrorist you are called!
That's your permanent label!
How beautiful your name!
Explain the ashes of destruction!
Over 3,000 body bags are empty and waiting!
You attacked the world, not the West!
You targeted your vile gutter warrior
misinterpretation of your sacredness!
You gained no friends, even in hell!

Educate us to the rationalization
of your vicious impotence!
There's no time to enter into negotiations!
Pay the world justice sentence
of your vicious crime!
Reform your hatred!
For our children's sake!
For your children's sake!
In the name of all!
In the name of Allah!
In the name of God!
Love knows no compromise!
Love knows no compromise!

Unpublished works

independence

some crazy white anglo-saxon yale-educated speechwriter
got high on some french acid in a conference of
the non-aligned nations and the western powers,
the president wanted a "liberation" speech, to compete
with mitterand and felipe gonzales, and to upstage
castro's inflammatory speech. the writer, high on street
mescaline, devised a wasp proposal (with-a-strong-parent)
which made the president look extremely
visionary: he announced that puerto rico will be given
independence, as a new democratic model. the speech received wonderful praise, the president encouraged the
speechwriter to draft "further plans" for the state dinner
speech. the writer got some mescaline and
drafted phase-in plans that would be sent to the american-
japanese industrial complex to make puerto rico a third-
world economic training base for manufacturing computer
software and the president immediately
conferred with the non-aligned for new military bases,
but the short range idea ran into trouble back at the pentagon, the chiefs of staff pressured the secretary of defense
to retain the commonwealth, why rock the boat. the
president decided to blame the speechwriter, who subsequently
got accepted into a drug program because he claimed that
some crazy puerto-rican-on-the-run-terrorist had given
him a leftist pill that drove him insanely to become an
agent for the socialist cause, but the crazy yale-educated
speechwriter who got high on mescaline, became a born-again
person and he never found out that it was a real puerto
rican movement, denouncing the executive council of the non-
aligned that had convinced the third-world nations to
refute any new agreements, that made the president rescind
his original independence offer.

guaguancó

singing coro, punto clave,
finger-snapping guagancó,
backwards jungles of Nigeria,
in new york they were transformed,

clave clave guaguancó
clave clave guaguancó

coro africano clave,
nuevo ritmo, new-found song,
abajo-down deep down on clave,
rhythms never be transformed.

clave clave guaguancó
clave clave guaguancó

bata drums, hand quinto clapping,
ritmo tumbadora noise,
chekere and warm palitos,
rené lópez in applause,

clave clave guaguancó
clave clave guaguancó

totico singing sonero,
coro rituals moving on,
batallando, castigando,
moving faster, junto al sol,

clave clave guaguancó, clave clave guaguancó,
clave clave guaguancó, clave clave guaguancó,

en los tiempos modernos de esta raza,
por los golpes trabajo de sudor,
combinamos la rumba tumbadora,
niches negros trigueños con el sol,

clave clave guaguancó, clave clave guaguancó,

armonía en la urbe 'to mezclada,
nuevos ritmos que alientan tú y yo,
africano mezclado en caribeño,
con los prietos puertorro de new york,

clave clave guaguancó, clave clave guaguancó,
clave clave guaguancó, clave clave guaguancó,

juntos en mano, ya marcando,
los pasillos de new york,
juntos en manos, comentando,
somos uno junto al son,

clave clave guaguancó, clave clave guaguancó,
clave, clave, clave, clave, clave, clave,
guaguancó, guaguancó, guaguancó, guaguancó.

cuentos to a lady singer, the moon

1
so sweet so gentle
rides the night
so sweet so gentle
gently she sings
between chords
of humanness
gently gently night
sings she sings

2
from far away I saw her part of me
yet so far away. somehow she was
of me somehow I was of her.
the church in her guitar was her smile
the conga in my spiritualism was my smile
two extremes became equal
the touch of the interaction
ended in full moon at midnight

3
the moon had a long blue dress
she made her face with a cloud
of mascara, the sun she shone
from east gave the moon's beauty
mark her smile, with so much light!
with so much light!

4
and the moon waltz
around the shadows
of my eyes, waltz ever
so slowly, waltz till dawn.

two friends in new york heat

that we can talk
with so little protection
and so much release
peels my skin raw

our eyes touched
the melting grounds
of spiritual imagery
and made love
in an intimate circle . . .
it was not enough, not yet

the eye of my i looked
at the you in me
and we intertwined
a melodious walk . . .   across the ghetto's arrabales
                          across the antiqued streets
                          across the ethnically accented
                                   touch of our smiles

and we ventured
into an adventure
not knowing where
it would take us
but, never mind
it didn't matter . . .
concentration of
our vibes were in
personal gender
intimate case

we traveled into
each other's intimacy
breaking the bonds
of friendship into
the fifth solitude

of developing passionate
love

                  our spirits had made orgasm
                  out of clouds in fountain dance
                  inside the meeting point of privacy
                  in between the waters of our tongues
                  seeming to imply amorous adjectives
                  inside the nudity of our bodies.
                  our spirits had coalesced
                  giving birth to two stars that must yet meet:
                  to produce physical rain
                  to give sun to a dying forest
                  to give the star's horoscope
                  its physical place on earth

that we can talk
with so little protection
and so much release
peels my skin raw

smile in remembrance of me

brothers, i died in silence—in screaming pain.
now i nod eternally, smile in remembrance of me.
my death was a young death, and my body full of
life still signs with the joy that all my good
friends are still alive.

hermanos, see my death with the complete relationship i had with thee. let this peace—piece
of telita be the thought of my death, to remind
you to look around before you go to sleep, to
see if someone needs help on the empty staircase.
smile in remembrance of me.

let this peace—piece of telita represent my love
for all of you. to the brothers i got high with
let the telita represent that;
overdose was not the cause of my death
the cause of my death is this society we live in
drugs is the international scheme of which i was
only the receptive receptor,
not the killer manipulator.

smile in remembrance of me.

i tried to expand. i tried to be, always some
kind of conflict pissed my daily being. i wanted
freedom, but was never given the chance, unless
i took a meaningless job doing something strange
to my being.

those that were with me around the time i died
i forgive.
they ran and left me there
i forgive.

while i stood in the empty hall
a star came shining in. there was a message, a
message that was not heard but through death it
was seen. i saw myself a savior for the call
of understanding. i became a martyr-third-generation
puertorriqueño asking you to ask yourself
the crucial question . . . why?

brothers, besides my action that caused my death
as you look at my casket, look at the beauty in
me which i saw of you

i love friendship. i was one for all

to santa barbara i prayed. her statue still flows
in my room, and now lies in my hands.
there is a feeling of emptiness in me.
i cannot produce a radiant smile again. please . . .
smile in remembrance of me

please! please brothers,
sisters, mamacitas,
please, please,
smile in remembrance of me.
throw a dance in my name.
at my death, i want to hear
all that was good in me that
will make you remember
raymond, ramoncito
a true brother of an alright guy

save this peace—piece of telita
so that i can hang around with you.

i leave you in talk
i see you from silence
come to my house to
sing the rosaries

say hello to willie colón
take these vibrations, fill
them with a smile and give
it back to me

as i depart, my death
was a necessity to
allow my spirit to
see the truth
as the truth is

smile in remembrance of me

Contents by Title